FOREWORD BY DR. SAMUEL PAGAN

ALTAR CALL

LESSONS ON SPIRITUAL RENEWAL BASED ON THE BOOK OF EZRA

DAN DE JESUS

KINGDOM PUBLISHING HOUSE

Altar Call
Lessons On Spiritual Renewal Based On The Book Of Ezra
© 2024 by Dan De Jesus

Unless otherwise marked, scriptures are taken from the HOLY BIBLE, NEW LIVING TRANSLATION, Copyright© 1996, 2004, 2007 by Tyndale House Foundation. Used by permission of Tyndale House Publishers, Inc., Carol Stream, Illinois 60188. All rights reserved. Used by permission.
Cover Design: QuezArt, Inc

Paperback ISBN-13: 979-898-54412-6-0
Hardcover ISBN-13: 979-821-84208-6-4
LCCN: 2022906498

Kingdom Publishing House
Long Island, New York

ENDORSEMENTS

"Pastor Dan's new book titled Altar Call will shake and stir you. His intuition and knowledge of the church's pulse today will help and guide you to God's presence. It's a piece of literature that should be read by every leader and pastor who is hungry to return to the altar."

Rev. Dr. Wilfredo De Jesús
General Treasurer,
Assemblies of God

"Dr. Daniel De Jesus has penned a resource that will help pastors and leaders navigate through the book of Ezra using a contemporary lens. He highlights several key concepts that serve as an evaluative tool for the discipleship of individuals. Thought-provoking questions will arise as you dive into the text, such as how can we identify spiritual slumber or disconnect? Have we become consumers of the gospel or disciples living on mission for God each day? I pray that as you journey through the book of Ezra using this resource, the Holy Spirit will ignite your personal altar and that a revival centered on God's Word will begin in your midst."

Rev. Elly C. Marroquin
National Director
Christian Education & Discipleship
The Assemblies of God

"The exposure of the sacred Scriptures is urgent for our generations. The preacher has the solemn responsibility of preaching "all of God's council." This work that you have in your hands exposes the book of Ezra. When was the last time you heard a series regarding this book? A lot is written about the book of Nehemiah, but expositions on the book of Ezra are limited. This is interesting given the fact that originally the book of Ezra was intertwined with the book of Nehemiah and was known as the book of Ezra-Nehemiah.

Dr. Daniel De Jesus offers a fresh and relevant exposition of this book, applying it to the church and the needs of the people of God today. The reading of this work will encourage the seeking of a personal revival. I strongly recommend the reading of this book."

Rev. Rafael Reyes
Superintendent Emeritus
Spanish Eastern District
Assemblies of God

"With great joy, I endorse this book that my colleague and friend, Rev. Dr. Daniel De Jesus--who I have known for over four decades--has written. I want to turn your attention to a very special man. His name is Ezra. His name means help. This book will help you greatly. First of all, Ezra is one of those fellows you do not hear a great deal about, yet he was a giant among men in the spiritual world.

This book will help you greatly in spiritual renewal and spiritual revitalization. All those who turn to God will experience a spiritual awakening. May the Lord continue to help you as you read the great principles found in the book of Ezra."

Rev. Manuel A. Álvarez
Superintendent
Spanish Eastern District
Assemblies of God

DEDICATION

THIS BOOK IS DEDICATED TO MY PARENTS, JULIO and Delia De Jesus, who rest in the arms of our Savior. They were great examples of how to live a Christian life near the altar. They bequeathed to me a legacy of worship and prayer that marked my life forever.

I also dedicate this book to my wife, Clarita, who has always supported me on every ministry assignment. My love, you are a great example of a woman of virtue. "The heart of her husband trusts in her."

Lastly, I dedicate this book to my children, Daniel, Cristian, and Jazmine. Always live near the altar. I love you all!

Dan De Jesus

TABLE OF CONTENTS

PROLOGUE

I AM MORE THAN HAPPY TO WELCOME YOU TO THE book of my esteemed colleague and friend, Dr. Daniel De Jesus. His works, which are nourished by his pastoral and academic experiences, manifest a relevant, healthy, pleasing, and challenging theology. It explores the important subject of the spiritual awakening grounded on the cautious reading of the book of Ezra. His main theological foundation is that God's people are in need of a spiritual awakening to exercise today's Christian mission.

According to our author, one of the elements of the restoration and returning of the people of Israel to Jerusalem was the divine revelation to Cyrus, the famous king of Persia. That special act allowed and encouraged the return of the people of God to the promised land. The "awakening" of the Persian monarch's heart is a symbol of what God is capable of doing in people and communities to affirm and manifest His will amongst life's realities.

As a divine answer to Cyrus's revelation, the Israelites decided to reconstruct the temple in Jerusalem, which was the optimum symbol of God's presence. That restoration, according to the biblical testimony, begins firm with the reconstruction of the altar. It is a fact that all personal and national restoration processes start soberly from the foundation of the altar in the temple.

Dr. De Jesus's writing in this book is of great importance because the whole world needs a "heart awakening," meaning a grand spiritual revival that will allow believers and the church to preach the gospel of Jesus Christ with value, effectiveness, dignity, and mercy. The twenty-first century needs a new revival to move the church and its leaders to accomplish the divine assignment to encourage and implement the spiritual, social, and educative processes that society needs. To fulfill these goals, which are based on faith, we must be "awakened" from the spiritual slumber that halts and disorients. In effect, we need to surpass the slumber that confuses and weakens the church and its leaders.

Pastor Daniel's book comes at a perfect time since we are rebuilding from a pandemic that greatly hurt the family and society and confused the mission of some believers and congregations. In the middle of all those challenges, Daniel surprises us with a new publication that interprets the biblical text in a creative form, thus effectively responding to the hardships we face. For our good friend, a true revival begins with an awakening in the heart that decides to restore God's altar; in other words, that commits to restructure the life founded on the grace and power of God.

I am thankful to Daniel for presenting this new book, which we deeply hope is a blessing for all of God's people.

Dr. Samuel Pagan
Dean of Hispanic Programs
Jerusalem Center for biblical Studies

1

A BROKEN WORLD
IN NEED OF REVIVAL

"Then God stirred the hearts of the priests and Levites and the leaders of the tribes of Judah and Benjamin to go to Jerusalem to rebuild the Temple of the Lord. And all their neighbors assisted by giving them articles of silver and gold, supplies for the journey, and livestock. They gave them many valuable gifts in addition to all the voluntary offerings." (Ezra 1:5-6)

I WANT TO ASK YOU A VERY IMPORTANT QUESTION:

How do you start your day?

If you are wise--and I believe you are--you start it with God. Talking to Him in prayer, spending some time in His Word, getting ready for whatever the day may bring.

I know from experience that this is the very best way for me to get off to a good start.

You may be thinking, "If this is the best way to start the day, then what's the worst?"

I can't speak for you, of course, but for me it's watching the morning news on television. When I do that, I hear about murders and other crimes, war in various parts of the world, about acts of hatred. This does not help me get off to a positive start on the day. Instead, it leaves me shaking my head and asking, "What's wrong with people?"

Of course, I already know the answer to my question. Simply put, people need God. They need to know that He is the creator of all life, that He loves His creatures with all of His being, and that He expects us to live in obedience to His commands. They have wandered away from Him and they need to come home.

Sometimes it seems to me that we are not far away from the days when God looked down on His creation and "observed the extent of human wickedness on the earth, and He saw that everything they thought or imagined was consistently and totally *evil*." (Genesis 6:5)

It was then that God wiped out most of life on the earth with a great flood – sparing only Noah and his family. But He promises us that this will not happen again. We serve a God who "does not want anyone to be destroyed, but wants everyone to repent." (2 Peter 3:9)

When Jesus was asked which is the greatest commandment in the Law of Moses, He replied:

> *"You must love the* LоRD *your God with all your heart, all your soul, and all your mind. This is the first and greatest commandment. A second is equally important: Love your neighbor as yourself. The entire law and all the demands of the prophets are based on these two command-ments."* (Matthew 22:36-40)

If everyone lived in obedience to these two laws, just imagine what a wonderful world this would be. If this were the case, I believe watching the morning news (or the evening news, for that matter) would be a great pleasure.

This broken world is desperately in need of a revival – and I believe that God is working through His people to make it happen.

As I look around me, I see that these are very difficult days for millions of people here in the United States and around the world. Many of us are plagued by uncertainty and fear. Our economy is unstable, often going up and down like a roller-coaster, and leaving us feeling insecure about our jobs and our future. We have recently passed through a life-changing disaster called COVID, the type of plague that we thought had been eradicated by modern science and medicine. We have been left reeling by dozens of mass shootings, many of which took place in our nation's schools. And, thousands of would-be immigrants are gathered at our borders, hoping to be let into the United States so they can escape the poverty and repression that exists in their home countries.

Like the ancient Israelites who were taken into captivity in Babylon, we are broken and bruised, and desperately in need of revival.

There have been dozens of great religious revivals throughout history. Hundreds of thousands of souls have been won to Christ and our entire societies were changed for the better. Revivals have produced opposition to slavery, brought legal protections for the poor, saved children's lives through child labor laws, etc. Every time the church is under attack, God sends revival.

For example, in the early days of the United States, it seemed that interest in "organized religion" had fallen off throughout the colonies. History.com says:

> "The Great Awakening was a religious
> revival that impacted the English colonies

in America during the 1730s and 1740s. The movement came at a time when the idea of secular rationalism was being emphasized, and passion for religion had grown stale. Christian leaders often traveled from town to town, preaching about the gospel, emphasizing salvation from sins and promoting enthusiasm for Christianity. The result was a renewed dedication toward religion. Many historians believe the Great Awakening had a lasting impact on various Christian denominations and American culture at large."[1]

One never knows how a revival will begin. Just as I started writing this book, a stirring revival took place at Asbury College in Kentucky. It began during a regularly scheduled chapel service on February 8, 2023. As time came for the service to be dismissed, nobody wanted to go home – so the revival continued. For the next two weeks, the auditorium was packed with thousands of people who worshiped God and basked in God's presence day and night. Most of these worshipers were students, but not all of them. In fact, as word spread that God was moving in a mighty way in Kentucky, people came from throughout the United States, and all over the world, to take part. By the time it all came to an end, some 50,000 to 70,000 visitors had come to Asbury to join

---

[1]   History.com/topics/European-history, "Great Awakening," by history.com editors, updated September 20, 2019

in the revival. Thousands of hearts were touched by the love and power of Jesus, and they will never be the same.

As I've said, there have been many such revivals in previous years. You never can tell when revival will break out. As Jesus said, " The wind blows wherever it wants. Just as you can hear the wind but can't tell where it comes from or where it is going, so you can't explain how people are born of the Spirit." (John 3:8)

In recent years, we have seen hundreds of thousands of men and women come to Jesus through the extraordinary preaching of men like Billy Graham and Luis Palau.

Most of us have heard of the Azusa Street Revival, which happened in Los Angeles in the early part of the 20th century. The revival stretched on for nearly ten years, during which many thousands of souls were won for Christ, and thousands of believers began to move in the supernatural gifts of the Holy Spirit. In fact, that revival is connected to the founding of the Assemblies of God, the denomination I serve as a pastor. Today, the Assemblies of God has an estimated 68 million members all over the world. I say this not to brag, but rather to show what can result from the fires of revival.

There have been other great revivals, of course. As I have already mentioned, The Great Awakening swept through the United States in the early days of the country, led by preachers like Jonathan Edwards and George Whitefield.

During this same time period, the Methodist Revival was burning brightly in England, thanks largely to the efforts of Brothers John and Charles Wesley.

There have been many other revivals throughout history, but it is not my intention to write a book on the history of revivals. Instead, I want to concentrate on one of the greatest revivals that has ever taken place--a revival led by a man named Ezra some 2,500 years ago. Ezra's work is recorded in the book of the Bible that bears His name--and it is just as pertinent today as it was then. Perhaps even more so, because our modern world is desperately in need of the type of revival that Ezra brought to the ancient Jews, many of whom had drifted away from their faith.

In this book, I will present a number of important lessons we can learn from the great revival of Ezra. This great man helped rekindle the fire of faith among the Jewish people who had suffered through 70 years of captivity. The entire nation responded to the call to come to the altar of God and rededicate their lives to the One who had brought them out of slavery in Egypt and established them in the Promised Land.

Today, God is calling us to come to His altar to meet with Him. He desires that all men and women everywhere would cleanse themselves in the blood of Jesus and live in holiness before Him.

As the apostle Paul said: "God overlooked people's ignorance about these things (sin) in earlier times, but now He commands everyone everywhere to repent of their sins and turn to Him." (Acts 17:30)

Now is the time to listen. Now is the time to respond. Now is the time to change our lives and our world.

Lesson #1 from the Book of Ezra

In the days of Ezra, God used the King of Persia to start bringing the Children of Israel back to their homeland after a lengthy exile. He always finds a way to accomplish good for believers who look to Him, though His methods may surprise us.

Submitting our lives into God's care means we can find peace, even in the most difficult times and situations. As Paul writes in Romans 8:28: "And we know that God causes everything to work together[for the good of those who love God and are called according to his purpose for them."

QUESTIONS FOR SPIRITUAL REFLECTION

1. Do you agree that revival is needed in the world today? Explain your answer.

____

____

____

2. Do you feel that you are personally in need of revival? Explain your answer.

____

____

____

3. Will you commit yourself to praying for revival on a regular basis?

____

____

____

4. What do you feel God is calling you to do to help
    bring about revival in yourself, your family, your
    church and your community?

____

____

____

2

EZRA TO THE RESCUE

This Ezra was a scribe who was well versed in the Law of Moses, which the LORD, the God of Israel, had given to the people of Israel. He came up to Jerusalem from Babylon, and the king gave him everything he asked for, because the gracious hand of the LORD his God was on him" (*Ezra 7:6*).

HAVE YOU EVER FELT THAT GOD HAS FORGOTTEN you?

I have.

And it is a very unpleasant feeling. I'm pretty sure that, if we were to be completely honest, we would all have to admit that at some time in our lives, we have felt like God has forgotten us. Even, Jesus, as he hung on the cross, cried out, "My God, my God, why have you forsaken me?" (Matthew 27:46) Of course, he was quoting the words of King David, from the first verse of the 22nd Psalm.

This feeling is common among baby Christians, who have received blessing after blessing, and miracle after miracle since they turned their lives over to Jesus. Then suddenly, the miracles stop. Instead of soaring to Heaven on the wings of Eagles, our prayers seem to flutter and fall back to earth like so many wounded ducks. What has happened?

The best explanation I have heard is that when we are first born again, God is like a loving Father, doing everything He can to help us grow in our faith. He holds our hand when we walk with Him. When we come to a dangerous place where we might fall and hurt ourselves, He picks us up and carries us.

Not long ago, I saw a father teaching his little girl how to ride a bicycle. Apparently, the training wheels had recently been removed. The bike was wobbly and seemed to be heading in several directions at once. But Dad was there, steadying the bike, grabbing the handlebars whenever necessary. As I watched them-- trying not to be too obvious about it--I thought, "That's exactly what God does for His children."

But sooner or later, He has to let go, or we'll never learn how to ride a bike on our own. Or handle a temptation the devil throws at us. Or stand strong when trouble comes our way, as it often does in this fallen world. God truly loves us, and He wants us to be all we are capable of being. He wants us to be strong and mature in Christ, and that will never happen if He coddles us every step of the way.

I don't know all the reasons why God sometimes seems distant. Sometimes it is due to our sin, but not always. Sometimes, there may be hard lessons He wants us to learn. Or, He may want to teach us how to walk by faith and not by sight.

But whatever the reason, two things are certain:

1) **God has not forgotten you.** Here is a sampling of what Jesus has to say about this:

> *"No, I will not abandon you as orphans—I will come to you. Soon the world will no longer see me, but you will see me. Since I live, you also will live"* (John 14:18-19).

> *". . . be sure of this: I am with you always, even to the end of the age"* (Matthew 28:20).

> *"I also tell you this: If two of you agree here on earth concerning anything you ask, my Father*

in heaven will do it for you. For where two or three gather together as my followers, I am there among them" (Matthew 18:19-20).

And Hebrews 13:5 tells us:

Don't love money; be satisfied with what you have. For God has said,

"I will never fail you.
I will never abandon you."

2) **It's not easy when you feel that He has withdrawn Himself from you.**

So imagine how it must have felt for the Jewish families who were taken into captivity in Babylon. They knew they were there because sin had come between them and their God. There was no doubt that He had sent foreign invaders into the land to punish the people for their transgressions. They had been dragged out of their homes, knowing that they would most likely never see them again. Even the beautiful temple, the center of worship for all Jews, had been destroyed. How could God do that? It was as if He had wiped away every bit of His connection with the Jewish people. Can you imagine the despair?

Fortunately, even though His judgment had fallen on the Children of Israel, he did not leave them alone. He sent them prophets like Jeremiah, Haggai and Zechariah to share His Word with them. He raised up mighty men of God like Daniel. (It was during the time of captivity that Daniel was delivered from the lion's den and that Daniel's friends were thrown into the fiery furnace, but came out completely unscathed.)

And then, just as God had chosen Moses to lead the Children of Israel out of Egypt, He raised up a number of heroes--like Ezra--to lead the people out of Babylon. They were given the task of taking the captives back to the Promised Land and repairing the damage that had been inflicted on the Holy City.

It has been many years since I first felt God planting within me the desire to write a book on the life of Ezra. This great Old Testament scribe and priest had a profound impact on the history of God's chosen people, the nation of Israel. You now hold in your hands the product of God's call for me to share the wisdom, joy and faith that comes from a study of Ezra's life.

Although Ezra is not one of the Old Testament's better-known heroes, I believe he is certainly one of the greatest. He never parted the Red Sea or brought water forth from a rock in the wilderness, but he is often referred to as the second Moses. After all, He was chosen by God to help nurture and restore the faith of the Jewish people after they had spent 70 years in captivity in Babylonia.

During those 70 years, Jerusalem had fallen into utter disrepair. After seven decades of neglect, almost nothing remained of the wall that once surrounded Jerusalem and protected her from her enemies, or Solomon's once-magnificent temple. The temple had suffered terribly at the hands of King Nebuchadnezzar, who had removed all the treasures from the temple in 604 and again in 597 B.C., and totally destroyed the building ten years after that. Even worse, God's Word had been lost and His people had succumbed to idolatry.

Ironically, the Jews who had been taken into captivity in Babylon fared much better than those who had been left behind in Judah. In Babylon, they lived in Jewish communities and were, for the most part, free to observe their religion. They had priests to teach them about God and lead them in worship. And they had the encouragement of prophets like Ezekiel, Haggai, Zechariah and, of course, Ezra.

I don't want to give you the impression that the Babylonians were benevolent. They were out to conquer the world and killed many thousands of men, women and children in the process. As the book of Daniel shows us, they also forced the people they had conquered to worship idols. It's just that they did not hate the Jews because of their ethnicity.

Perhaps you've heard it said that King Frederick the Great of Prussia once asked his physician to give him proof for the existence of God. His physician smiled and answered quickly, "The continued existence of the Jews, your Majesty."

He got it right. It is indeed amazing that the Jewish people, who have endured thousands of years of persecution, have survived to this very day. All of the other nations that are listed in the Old Testament as rivals of the ancient Israelites have faded into history. The Philistines. The Amalekites. The Ishmaelites. The Ninevites. Not a single one of them remain.

Except the Jews. And Ezra had an extremely important role in making their survival possible. He was one of the great men God used to restore and purify the Jewish nation, and thus prepare the way for the arrival of the Messiah, Jesus Christ.

As far as I can remember, I've never before seen a book on the life of Ezra. There are dozens of books on Moses, Paul, David, Nehemiah, Abraham, and other heroes of the Bible, but Ezra seems to have passed almost unnoticed. He has so much to teach us, yet many turn away and look for someone more exciting.

I was deeply stirred as I followed God's calling and immersed myself in the book of Ezra. I could clearly see this ancient story of Israel relived in the hearts of so many who struggle to connect with the heart of our heavenly

Father today. As a Pastor, I desire to see God's people enter their best season. My hope is for all who have confessed Jesus Christ as their Savior to experience a season of glory as they encounter God in a fresh and new way. Ezra has much to teach those who are willing to open their ears and hearts.

Who Was Ezra?

Ezra was a descendent of Aaron, Moses' brother who served as a chief priest during the Israelites exodus from Egypt, and was also related to Joshua, who succeeded Moses as leader of Israel. In addition to writing the book that bears his name, he also contributed to both 1st and 2nd Chronicles, and is believed to be the author of one of the most beautiful and powerful of the Psalms, Psalm 119.

In about 538 B.C., King Cyrus proclaimed that God's temple in Jerusalem was to be rebuilt, and the first group of volunteers left Babylon for the 700-mile journey back to the Promised Land.   Unfortunately, these brave men encountered opposition from those who did not want to see Israel rise up from the ashes, and it took nearly 30 years to complete the job.

Ezra 6:15 says, "The temple was completed on March 12, during the sixth year of King Darius's reign." Ezra himself was in another group that was sent back to Jerusalem by the next king, Artaxerxes. When he reached the city, he found that the temple had been restored and was standing tall and proud. But in many ways, the beautiful building was nothing more than a façade. The symbol of worship had been restored--but the people did not worship God as they once had.

Tragically, the Jews who remained in Israel had not kept themselves separate from the heathen tribes, as God had commanded them. Instead, they had inter-married with these tribes and had incorporated some of their detestable practices into their own worship. (Some Israelites even went so far as to sacrifice their babies to the Canaanite God Molech, which meant that they were offered alive as burnt sacrifices.) When told of the peo-ple's sin, Ezra immediately tore his cloak and sat down. Later, he rose to his knees and prayed out to God for for-giveness. Afterwards, he issued a call for all the exiles to gather in the city, where he directed the men to separate from their foreign wives and children.

Ezra encourages us to stand up for our faith. He knew that the Torah had been neglected and forgotten by many during the Jewish exile. So in Jerusalem, he spoke boldly and forcefully about the importance of obeying God's laws. It broke his heart to see that the Jewish people had forgotten that they were God's chosen people. They were supposed to be a unique people, but they had completely forgotten their wonderful heritage.

In the Hebrew Bible, Ezra and Nehemiah were pre-sented as one book, and can still be read that way. Because the prophets Haggai and Zechariah also ministered in Jerusalem during this time period, the books that bear their names compliment the book of Ezra. All of them emphasize the restoration of the nation's physical and spiritual life.

As we've already discussed, the book of Ezra contains the story of one of the most amazing awakenings of ancient Israel. It's the story of a nation that returns to God after seventy years in captivity. In fact, the people of the great I AM had lived so many years under captivity that they grew accustomed to slavery and deprivation. This was their normal way of life.

Tragically, many of God's children live under the same circumstances today. They sleep-walk through their days, feeling that their lives don't have any purpose. They drag their burdens around as if there were no way to break free from a mindset that is marked by lethargy and indifference.

Many have slipped into a state of slumber (more on this in Chapter Three). They've abandoned their altar, the place of surrender, renewal and revival. All that remains are the ashes of the fire that once burned brightly, but then slowly died out, and left us with nothing to hold onto but nostalgia for what used to be. Pentecost Sunday has become a day we simply commemorate but no longer live out daily. This is precisely why God is calling His people, a nation of true worshippers, to seek him in spirit and in truth.

Faith is not the same as sentimentality. Far from it.

You may know people who get misty-eyed when they hear the old songs that Grandma used to sing. Like "The Old Rugged Cross," or "What a Friend We Have in Jesus." But are their tears for Christ's agony on the cross, or do they merely represent a longing for the "good old days." There's nothing wrong with these old hymns. I love many of them myself. But we must not equate the nostalgic longing for the church we attended as a child with our love for Jesus Christ. They are not the same thing, and if we are not careful, our longing for that old church we used to attend (or any such aspect of our Christian faith) will supplant our love for and faith in Jesus Christ.

Sentimental people tend to live in the past. They long for the good old days, and are not happy about all the innovations that have come into the modern worship service--such as worship bands. Their motto is, "But we've never done it this way before." But true faith is always marching forward to win the world for Christ. When I think of people of faith, I think of those who have been baptized in water and the Spirit, men and women filled with Holy Ghost fire who demonstrate the power of God in their actions and deeds. They are fully alive and fully awake. They are storming the gates of hell, not hiding in fear behind locked doors.

As you read the first chapter of the book of Ezra, you'll learn how God began to awaken his people after they had been held captive for so many years. God called out to His people by using an ungodly man, King Cyrus, who did not serve Him but was in a position of power and could provoke a season of change to a nation that had drifted away from Him. They couldn't hear God themselves because they were in a deep slumber. When God has a purpose with a person or group of people, He will do whatever it takes, use whomever He pleases, and do anything necessary to get His children's attention.

The king of Persia didn't serve the God of Israel; nevertheless, his heart was sensitive to God's calling.

The Bible tells us, "In the first year of King Cyrus of Persia, the LORD fulfilled the prophecy he had given through Jeremiah. He stirred the heart of Cyrus to put this proclamation in writing and to send it throughout his kingdom:" (Ezra 1:1)

If we look up this same verse in other Bible versions, we will find the following:

The New Living Bible says, "The Lord *worked* in the spirit."

The New International Version reads, "The Lord *moved* the heart of Cyrus king of Persia."

And **The Voice** has it as, "The Eternal One *influenced* the spirit of the Persian king."

It doesn't matter which version you read. God is currently stirring, working, moving, and influencing the hearts of his children so that they will turn back to the heart of the Father. `

You see, King Cyrus represents *us* today, and if God *stirred* his heart, it means there are people today living under unrest and anxiety who need to hear God's voice in order to regain their place in His kingdom. The word *stirring* in Hebrew is Qu`wr, and it means to awaken, arouse, or excite, and it's what God is doing right now![2]

What was it like for the Jewish exiles living in Babylonia. I love these words from Eugene Peterson's classic book, *Run with the Horses:*[3]

> *"The essential meaning of exile is that we are not where we want to be. We are separated from home. We are not permitted to reside in*

---

[2]   https://www.bibletools.org/index.cfm/fuseaction/Lexicon.show/ID/H5782/%60uwr.htm

[3] Eugene H. Peterson, "Run with the Horses," (InterVarsity Press; Downer's Grove, Ill.) 1983, Page 148

the place where we comprehend and appreciate our surroundings. We are forced to be away from that which is most congenial to us. It is an experience of dislocation--everything is out of joint; nothing fits together. The thousand details that have been built up through the years that give a sense of at-homeness—-gestures, customs, rituals, phrases—are all gone. Life is ripped out of the familiar soil of generations of language, habit, weather, story-telling and rudely and unceremoniously dropped into some unfamiliar spot on earth. The place of exile may boast a higher standard of living. It may be more pleasant in its weather. That doesn't matter. It isn't home."

Peterson also writes:[4]

Exile is traumatic and terrifying. Our sense of who we are is very much determined by the place we are in and the people we are with.

When that changes, violently, abruptly, who are we? The accustomed ways we have of finding our worth and sensing our significance vanish. The first wave of emotion recedes and leaves us feeling worthless, meaningless. We don't fit in anywhere. No one expects us to do anything.

---

[4] Ibid, Page 147

No one needs us. We are extra baggage. We aren't necessary."

He paints a pretty bleak picture of life in exile. Babylonia may not have been the worst place in the world to relocate to. But going there was still a traumatic, life-changing event for the descendants of Abraham. Their country had been defeated by a foreign enemy. The temple of God had been destroyed. Could anything be worse?

Shaken, not stirred

I am deeply saddened that many of us today don't seem to mind living in exile. We have been separated from God, not by a powerful enemy, but by our own indifference and apathy. What a tragedy to be living in the shadows rather than in the light of God's love.

When I was a young man, one of my favorite fictional characters was Ian Fleming's British secret agent *James Bond 007*. His catchphrase to describe the preparation of his signature cocktail was *"Shaken, not stirred."*[5] I find that today many of God's people prefer the same experience, where they are shaken emotionally or simply motivated but not one in which they are awakened spiritually. They don't mind being moved emotionally. In fact, they demand it from their pastors. They want a bit of a tug on the heartstrings, and may even enjoy shedding a tear

---

[5] https://en.wikipedia.org/wiki/Shaken,_not_stirred

or two once in a while. But they don't want to be provoked into putting their lives on the line for the sake of the kingdom.

We attend service after service and conference after conference, only to be shaken but not stirred, *shaken but not awakened!* In the last video of perhaps the greatest evangelist of our time, Billy Graham said the following: *"There have been moments where I have cried while traveling from city to city, seeing how far people have wandered from God."* And then he went on to say, *"Our nation has a great need for a spiritual awakening."*[6] There is an awakening that will sweep across the globe like never before, and we're privileged to be alive to see the next great move of God. God is awakening His church for such a time as this.

---

[6]   https://www.usatoday.com/story/news/politics/2013/11/07/billy-graham-95th-birthday-party-final-sermon/3464537/

Lesson #2 from the Book of Ezra

Have you ever considered what Ezra gave up when he returned from Babylon to Jerusalem? Babylon was a world power, a country with all the modern conveniences. Jerusalem, on the other hand, had been devastated by her enemies. Yes, the Jewish people had been taken to Babylon as captives. But they had followed the advice of the prophet Jeremiah and had planted gardens, built homes, and worked "for the peace and prosperity of the city where I sent you into exile" (Jeremiah 29:7) As a priest and scribe, Ezra was a leader in the Jewish community. He was certainly leaving the good life behind when he returned to Jerusalem. What about us? May God grant that we will be like Ezra, ready to give up everything for the sake of God's kingdom.

QUESTIONS FOR SPIRITUAL REFLECTION

1. What is the condition of your altar today?

2. Do you feel there are still areas in your life that need to be surrendered to God?

3. What challenges are hindering you from drawing closer to God?

4. Have you felt God's calling in your life?

____

31

____

____

5. Are there areas of your life where you need to be shaken <u>and</u> stirred? Explain your answer,

____

____

____

3

THE GREAT AWAKENING

In the first year of King Cyrus of Persia, the Lord *fulfilled the prophecy he had given through Jeremiah. He stirred the heart of Cyrus to put this proclamation in writing and to send it throughout his kingdom:*

"This is what King Cyrus of Persia says:

"'The Lord*, the God of heaven, has given me all the kingdoms of the earth. He has appointed me to build him a Temple at Jerusalem, which is in Judah.'"*

I SAID EARLIER THAT FAR TOO MANY BELIEVERS ARE sleepwalking through their days. Perhaps you have heard it said that people normally pass through four stages when we sleep.[7] The first stage is the lightest stage. This drowsy sleep stage can be easily disrupted, causing awakenings or arousals. Our muscle tone throughout the body relaxes, and brain wave activity decreases. You might consider it to be a stage of pre-sleep, for the second of the four stages is actually the first stage of sleep. Awakenings or arousals do not occur as easily as in stage one. Brain waves continue to decelerate, body temperature begins to decrease, and the heart rate starts to slow down. Stage three is known as deep sleep. Awakenings or arousals are rare and it is often difficult to awaken someone in this stage.

Parasomnias, such as sleepwalking, sleep talking, or nightmares, occur during this deep stage of sleep. The fourth and final stage is the REM sleep stage, also known as rapid eye movement, and it's most commonly known as the dreaming stage. However, awakenings and arousals can occur more easily in the REM stage.

These four stages are comparable to those we may go through in a spiritual sense, because spiritual slumber is a condition of the soul.

- In stage one, we begin to relax, and our ability to discern decreases.

---

[7] https://www.verywellhealth.com/
the-four-stages-of-sleep-2795920

- In stage two, our hearts lose their passion for our walk with God. What we used to consider wrong behavior loses its pre-established boundaries. Our spiritual heart rate decreases to the point that we have slowly disconnected from our relationship with God.

- In the third stage, we slip into a deep stage of sleep where what we say no longer makes any sense; we're just talking in our sleep, and nothing we say is clear.

- And finally, in stage four, we are completely disconnected and unaware of our surroundings, having entered our own reality. We no longer feel anything because we're dreaming. Sadly, this illustrates the spiritual condition of many of God's people today.

Sleep Can Be a Blessing

Sleep is vital to the health of our body and spirit. I think of Jesus peacefully asleep in a small fishing boat caught in the grip of a terrible storm on the Sea of Galilee. The apostles were completely panicked, but Jesus knew the situation was safely in His Father's hands (Luke 8:22-25). If you've ever been in an airplane being tossed around by turbulence, you may have some idea of how the apostles felt in the middle of that storm.

It is a blessing to be able to sleep peacefully in the arms of God no matter what is happening all around us--but there is a time to sleep and a time to be wide awake.

There are so many blessings from God that Satan has twisted into dangerous threats against us. I think of the computer, for example. Computers have blessed our lives in so many ways. Thanks to the computer we have whole worlds of information at our fingertips. We can instantly communicate immediately with people anywhere in the world. And computers have made a tremendous difference for writers. You no longer have to cut and paste when you've made a typo, or crumple up a page and throw it in the trash because you've made a major mistake. It's easy to go back and erase the mistake and then keep going.

But for all the good things they've brought us, computers are also responsible for many modern heartbreaks. Identity theft has become a billion-dollar business and cyber-criminals are largely responsible. Thousands of innocent people have lost their life savings to computer-generated scams, and it's a tragedy. Computers have also brought access to pornography into our homes, which has led to sex addictions and broken up countless families. And it has allowed the bullies among us to spew their hatred and vitriol any time they desire. Who knew there were so many hateful "trolls" all around us?

As I said earlier, whenever we read of some new invention that is full of potential to help humankind, we can be sure the devil will find a way to twist it to hurt us. That's what he does!

For example, no human life can survive without water, and yet thousands of lives are lost to drowning every year. Fire provides us with warmth on cold winter nights. But if fire gets out of control, it can destroy entire communities. Nuclear energy can provide an abundant supply of inexpensive electrical power. But used in the wrong way, nuclear power has the potential to destroy the entire world. It's difficult to think of a good gift God has given us that the devil has not twisted and tried to use against us.

And so it is with sleep. Sleep can restore our energy, giving us the strength to do what God has called us to do. But too much sleep can dull the senses and blind us to God's call on our life. Consider Peter, John and James, who were asked by the Lord to watch and pray with Him as he faced arrest on the night of His betrayal. One hour was all He asked of these dear friends of His, but because of the power sleep had over them, they could not do it. The tragic story is found in the 26th Chapter of Matthew:

> *Then Jesus went with them to the olive grove*
> *called Gethsemane, and he said, "Sit here*
> *while I go over there to pray." He took Peter*
> *and Zebedee's two sons, James and John, and*

he became anguished and distressed. He told them, "My soul is crushed with grief to the point of death. Stay here and keep watch with me."

He went on a little farther and bowed with his face to the ground, praying, 'My Father! If it is possible, let this cup of suffering be taken away from me. Yet I want your will to be done, not mine."

Then he returned to the disciples and found them asleep. He said to Peter, 'Couldn't you watch with me even one hour? Keep watch and pray, so that you will not give in to temptation. For the spirit is willing, but the body is weak!"

Then Jesus left them a second time and prayed, "My Father! If this cup cannot be taken away unless I drink it, your will be done." When he returned to them again, he found them sleeping, for they couldn't keep their eyes open.

So he went to pray a third time, saying the same things again. Then he came to the disciples and said, 'Go ahead and sleep. Have your rest. But look—the time has come. The Son of Man is betrayed into the hands of sinners. Up, let's be going. Look, my betrayer is here!'"
(Verses 36-46)

The Stirring of the Church of Sardis

Perhaps the best example in Scripture of a church that was found to be spiritually dead or asleep is the church of Sardis. In the Book of Revelation, Jesus quickly and clearly condemned their state of slumber. He told them, "I know all the things you do, and that you have a reputation for being alive—but you are dead. Wake up! Strengthen what little remains, for even what is left is almost dead. I find that your actions do not meet the requirements of my God. Go back to what you heard and believed at first; hold to it firmly. Repent and turn to me again. If you don't wake up, I will come to you suddenly, as unexpected as a thief" (Revelation 3:1-3).

Spiritual slumber occurs when our affection for the past become greater than our excitement for the future. We have become nostalgic in our walk with God, and it's a walk based on memories, but with no inspiration for the present day. The church at Sardis may have had a good reputation, but they were spiritually lifeless. In other words, these people were going through the motions of religion. Jesus then called them to repent of their sin, to wake up and start paying attention to their need of salvation, to stop being careless about their heart's condition before God.

Spiritual slumber also occurs when we are more concerned about our reputation than our mission. The church at Sardis had maintained a reputation of being alive, even though they were dead. It's as if they were pouring their energy into maintaining their reputation to their neighbors and neglecting their call to preach the gospel that awakens the soul. They were more focused on how they were being perceived than on their mission, to win their neighbors to Jesus.

Our desire to impact our world socially does not supersede our condition before God spiritually. We can't hide behind our profile picture forever; Jesus sees the real you!

There's a place and time to look back and celebrate the things God has done, but we cannot solely look to past inspirations for present-day motivations.

Finally, Sardinians had adopted a consumer mentality instead of a servant's heart. It's possible that in their heyday, they had grown so large that they turned their focus inward to manage and protect what they had accomplished. As a result, they became cautious, territorial, and perhaps took very little risks and stopped innovating for the sake of the gospel. They began to focus on pleasing the congregation rather than reaching their community. It became all about "me" instead of the lost "them" in the community. Jesus is calling the church to awaken from their slumber and seek him afresh every day.

What's interesting is that Sardinians had a history of complacency that plagued them. Sardis was once the ancient capital of the Lydian kingdom and was ruled by an extremely wealthy king named Croesus. In his pride, Croesus launched an attack against Cyrus, king of Persia, but was defeated in battle. He later returned to Sardis to regroup and rebuild an army, only to discover that the entire Persian army was mounting their own counterattack. At the time, the main city was on an acropolis about 1,500 feet high. It is said that in their pride, the Sardinians couldn't imagine anyone scaling their high walls to enter the city. So complacency crept in, and security became very lax. The watchmen on the towers became less vigilant and apparently fell asleep.   Unfortunately, their misguided complacency led to an invasion as skilled Persian climbers easily scaled their walls and invaded the city.[8]

Now, here's what's really sad about this story. It happened twice in the history of Sardis. The first occurred sometime in 549 BC with King Cyrus and the Persians. The second time around was three centuries later, in 195 BC, when Antiochus the Great conquered the city through the exact same strategy (his soldiers climbed up the walls undetected). The Sardinians had a culture of slumber, one that would eventually lead to their demise.[9]

When Jesus called the church in that city to snap out of their spiritual slumber, it wasn't a gentle plea. He was

---

[8] https://lineagejourney.com/read/sardis-the-dead-church

[9] ibid

screaming at the top of His lungs, "Wake up! Strengthen what little remains, for even what is left is almost dead. I find that your actions do not meet the requirements of my God" *(Revelation 3:2)*.

Stirred by the Word

Only the Word of God can stir the soul in ways nothing else can. Hebrews 4:12 tells us, "For the word of God is alive and powerful. It is sharper than the sharpest two-edged sword, cutting between soul and spirit, between joint and marrow. It exposes our innermost thoughts and desires." There is hope and that hope is found in the one thing that awakens the soul, and that is the obedience to God's Word.

King Cyrus was stirred by the fulfillment of a word given to Jeremiah, "For the time is coming when I will restore the fortunes of my people Israel and Judah. I will bring them home to this land that I gave to their ancestors and they will possess it again. I, the Lord, have spoken!" *(Jeremiah 30:3)* Jeremiah's prophecy would be fulfilled in the days of King Cyrus.

Only God's Word can stir the soul to awaken it from its slumber. For this reason, Jesus told the Sardinians, "Go back to what you heard and believed at first; hold to it firmly. Repent and turn to me again. If you don't wake up, I will come to you suddenly, as unexpected as a thief" (Rev. 3:3). Awakening from a spiritual slumber would require a return back to the basics of the faith, which are "heard and believed." Jesus exhorted them to "hold to it firmly," which simply means to do what it says.

In the chapters that follow, we will elaborate more on the things that we have "received and heard." This simply means that you need to go back and do the things that stirred your affections for Christ when you first became a Christian. I'm not speaking of the superficial things that were just emotion-based but concrete biblical activities that reveal God in all His glory.

When my faith felt like it was waning, I've found that returning back to fasting and prayer often stirs my affections and grows my love for Jesus Christ. For others, it may mean you start by going back and prayerfully rereading the Gospels so that you see Jesus Christ anew.

Lastly, fundamental to our faith is our understanding about the meaning of true repentance. Jesus called the Sardinians to repent from their slumber to experience a true revival. Over the years, I've heard so much about revival that it has become just another word that excites the church, but was never accompanied with real transformation. I'm talking about the kind of transformation the apostle Paul mentions in his letter to the early church in Corinth. "So all of us who have had that veil removed can see and reflect the glory of the Lord. And the Lord--who is the Spirit--makes us more and more like him as we are changed into his glorious image" (2 Corinthians 3:18).

Repentance has always been the place where we begin to find our way back to restoring our relationship with God. Only through our acknowledgment of where we are can we be propelled to where we need to be.

The time has come for God's people to return to the place of spiritual renewal that will allow for the church, the house of God, to be restored. Ezra 1:5 states, "Then God stirred the hearts of the priests and Levites and the leaders of the tribes of Judah and Benjamin to go to Jerusalem to rebuild the Temple of the LORD." There is a remnant, a new generation of believers whose soul God is stirring to return and take their rightful place here on earth. My prayer is that our hearts are stirred by God's Word to return to a place of true repentance to experience true renewal. Let the church arise and return in this final hour!

Altar Call

The main reason God stirred or moved the heart of King Cyrus was so he could be the instrument between God's people and the calling to return and rebuild the altar and the temple that had been in ruins. There are several details that tie into this calling from God that reveals what the Holy Spirit wishes to do today.

God requested the reconstruction of the temple in Jerusalem, specifically in the territory of Judah. Judah means praise. Therefore, God was demanding his children to return to a place of worship. It is through praise and worship that we can connect directly to the heart of the Father. When we enter the stages of somnolence, the first area to reflect decay is worship. Little by little, silence begins to dominate. Sadness, anxiety, fear, and the distance created between God begins to extinguish our worship. King David was able to recognize this, and when it came to the point in which he wasn't able to praise, he ordered his soul to worship: "Let all that I am praise the LORD; with my whole heart, I will praise his holy name. Let all that I am praise the LORD; may I never forget the good things he does for me" (Psalm 103:1–2). God could have requested a new altar built in a new territory, but He spoke clearly, stating it needed to be in the territory of Judah--in worship. God desires to enthrone himself in his children's worship. There are altars (hearts) in ruins in which worship no longer exists, and we must rebuild those places of worship if revival is to take place within us.

Another detail that cannot be overlooked is that King Cyrus made two stipulations in his decree, and the children of Israel had two choices:

> *"Any of you who are his people may go to Jerusalem in Judah to rebuild this Temple of the LORD, the God of Israel, who lives in Jerusalem. And may your God be with you! Wherever this Jewish remnant is found, let their*

> *neighbors contribute toward their expenses by giving them silver and gold, supplies for the journey, and livestock, as well as a voluntary offering for the Temple of God in Jerusalem"* (Ezra 1:3-4).

The Jews in Babylonia had to decide if they wanted to remain there or return to Jerusalem and rebuild what had been destroyed. Keep in mind that remaining meant living under the same conditions of captivity they had become accustomed to. The open call to return to Jerusalem meant leaving everything they knew behind and moving to a land many had never seen. Not everyone responded to God's calling.

In the same way, many of us today have become so accustomed to bondage that we run from away liberty. We embrace sadness because we don't know how to manage happiness.

God is knocking at the door of His children's hearts, but it's up to us to decide if we let Him in or if He remains outside. Sometimes we pray for a revival, but we are so used to the earthly way of living that we have lost sight of the spiritual things that connect us to God. The altar call is not just to reconcile a heart to God, but also to activate those responses God is demanding from us.

Even in this open decree that the king allowed, there were two options. The first was to return and help rebuild

God's temple, and the other was to economically support the men of God who were carrying out the work. The decree was clear: *"And in any locality where survivors may now be living, the people are to provide them with silver and gold, with goods and livestock, **and with freewill offerings for the temple of God in Jerusalem**." (Ezra 1:4, emphasis added).*

We preach and state that we are aware of the Great Commission to preach the gospel all around the world, but we are unable or unwilling to support ministries that live by faith or people who serve as missionaries in countries and territories that few are brave enough to visit. Ironically, those who are not members of God's people (or of the Church) are often more supportive and generous.

The first chapter in the book of Ezra makes clear that the ones who were leading the group that went back to Jerusalem were from the tribes of Judah and Benjamin. In times when the tabernacle carried the presence of God, the tribe of Judah was positioned in the front at the entry, and the tribe of Benjamin was positioned in the back of the tabernacle. The worship leaders were mainly from the tribe of Judah, and the warriors from the tribe of Benjamin. God is calling back the worshipers and prayer warriors.

Another important lesson we learn is that when God stirred Cyrus's heart and the king sent out a decree that would lead to the reconstruction of the temple, he also returned everything that Nebuchadnezzar had stolen from the temple.

There is an important lesson to be learned from this, and it is that when God calls you to come back to the altar--to your permanent safe place, everything the enemy took from you will be returned.

You may remember the story of Job, from the Old Testament book that bears his name. If so, you will recall that Satan took everything from Job, except his life. He lost his sons and daughters, his property, his crops, his livestock, and even his health. (He would have taken Job's life, were it not for the fact that God expressly forbade him to do so.) He was in constant pain, and his wife urged him to "curse God and die."

But when Job persevered in the midst of his trial, and told his wife and his friends that he would trust God no matter what, everything he had lost was restored to him. The Bible says:

> *After Job had prayed for his friends, the* LORD *restored his fortunes and gave him twice as much as he had before. All his brothers and sisters and everyone who had known him before came and ate with him in his house. They comforted and consoled him over all the trouble the* LORD *had brought on him, and each one gave him a piece of silver and a gold ring.*

*The Lord blessed the latter part of Job's life more
than the former part. He had fourteen thousand
sheep, six thousand camels, a thousand yoke
of oxen and a thousand donkeys. And he also
had seven sons and three daughters. The first
daughter he named Jemimah, the second Keziah
and the third Keren-Happuch. Nowhere in all
the land were there found women as beautiful as
Job's daughters, and their father granted them
an inheritance along with their brothers.*

*After this, Job lived a hundred and forty years;
he saw his children and their children to the
fourth generation.* ¹⁷ *And so Job died, an old
man and full of years"* -- Job 42:10-17.

How far will you obey?

Ever since I gave my life to Jesus Christ, I have tried my
best to obey him. As I look back on my life, I see occasions
when obedience was a real struggle. To be honest, I didn't
always want to obey. But I can see that when I did, God
worked it out for my benefit and His glory. On the occasions where I dug my heels in and pretended not to hear
what He was telling me, I came to regret it with all my
heart. Why? Not because He punished me, but because
I missed out on His best for. Plus, I know it hurts Him
when we don't obey, and hurting my Lord is the last thing
I ever want to do.

Still, I wonder sometimes how far my obedience would go. How about you? Would you do what Ezra did and give up a good life in Babylon to go back and help rebuild devastated Jerusalem? Would you do what Abraham did, when he prepared to give up his son, Isaac, as a sacrifice to the Lord? Could you pack up all your belongings and take your family off to a land you've never seen before, like Abraham did?

I hope I would obey the Lord no matter what. But you never really know what you would do until you are put in the position of saying "Yes, Lord," or "Lord, please find someone else." I feel certain that I would obey the Lord if I felt it would make me look like a hero. But what if it would make me look silly? What if people laughed at me? That would probably be harder to take.

Standing on your head for God

I recently read about a woman--let's call her Susan--who was driving past a convenience store when she felt the Lord directing her: "I want you to go into that store and stand on your head."

At first, she laughed it off, thinking, "I must be imagining things."

But the feeling wouldn't let her go. And, as a matter of fact, Susan felt that she was supposed to do it so that the sales clerk could see her. As you can guess by what

I've said so far, Susan is a strong believer in Jesus Christ and had learned to listen for His leading.

She circled the block a couple of times while she argued with the Lord, but finally gave in. She found a parking space and went into the store. The store wasn't busy, but there were a couple of customers. Susan pretended to be browsing until they finally left. She looked around and saw that the place was empty. This was her chance.

She called out to the sales clerk, who stood behind the cash register, "Hey, watch this!"

She quickly stood on her head, and then got back up on her feet. Much to her surprise, the clerk didn't laugh or say, "What do you think you're doing?" Instead, she began to cry. Big, glistening tears rolled down her cheeks.

"I'm sorry," Susan said. "I didn't mean to upset you. Please don't cry."

"It's not that," the clerk gulped through her tears.

"What then?"

The woman explained that she was going through a very difficult time in her life. She felt that nobody loved her, not even God. She had even begun to doubt his existence. She began contemplating taking her own life, but then she made a request of God:

"If you're really there and you really care about me, I want you to send someone into the store, and have them stand on their head in front of me."

It was a crazy request to be sure. And I would never recommend putting God to the test that way. But He is able to do anything, and He went to great lengths to show His love. Thank Goodness Susan was listening. That one "silly" thing Susan was willing to do changed the clerk's life with the love of Jesus.

May we all listen, and be ready to do whatever God commands!

Lesson #3 from the Book of Ezra

In the time of Ezra, many Jews had become separated from God. They had never heard His Word. They were desperately in need of the revival that God brought them through men like Ezra. Similarly, in the early 1700s, the American church was--for the most part--spiritually dead. The colonists were becoming wealthy, comfortable and self-satisfied. As faith dimmed, many churches lowered their standards for membership. You no longer had to be a Christian to be a church member. A "great awakening" was needed--and God brought it about through preachers like Jonathan Edwards, George Whitefield and Theodorus Frelinghuysen. These men began preaching powerful sermons directly from the Word of God. They shared about the necessity of having a personal relationship with Christ. And revival exploded across the colonies. These are the keys we must use to spur revival in the 21st century: The Word of God and the power of a personal relationship with Christ. When we share these things, revival is sure to follow.

QUESTIONS FOR SPIRITUAL REFLECTION

1. What steps can we take to remain completely awake and vital in our Christian walk.

2. If you had been living in Babylonia at the time of Ezra, do you think you would have gone back to Jerusalem or stayed in captivity? Explain your answer.

3. "It is through praise and worship that we can connect directly to the heart of the Father." Do you live a life-style of praise and worship?

____

____

____

4. What has the enemy taken from you that you would like to have returned?

____

____

____

4

ARISE AND ASCEND

"Now these are the people of the province who came up from the captivity of the exiles, whom Nebuchadnezzar king of Babylon had taken captive to Babylon (they returned to Jerusalem and Judah, each to their own town. . ." (Ezra 2:1)

THROUGHOUT THE SCRIPTURES, WE CONSTANTLY see a Heavenly Father who goes after His lost children. The desire of his heart is for His children to want to love, worship, and have an intimate relationship with Him. God told Jeremiah before the initial captivity: *"So the Lord says, 'If you return, then I will let you take your place again, standing before Me.'"* (Jeremiah 15:19, NASB 1995) Even before this captivity, God was calling his people to return to him. The Lord continued to come near His people and call their attention through His mercy and grace. No matter where we may have stumbled or fallen, the Heavenly Father is calling us to arise and ascend back to our rightful place by His side. This is where we belong—in the safe fold our Father has prepared for us since before the beginning of time.

Despite God's loving call, His people were still not willing to return and live under His will and ways. For this reason, He delivered them into the hands of the Babylonians. Seventy years had gone by when this calling to return to Jerusalem took place so that the Temple could be restored. The reconstruction of the Temple was God's way of reviving his people.

The decision to reconstruct requires commitment and courage. For those who obeyed God's call to return to Jerusalem, it would mean leaving behind the land of Babylonia that, for many, was their place of birth and upbringing. Very few people who entered Babylonia under the initial captivity were still alive. Many were born into this scenario. Babylonia was their home, and they had no recollection of Jerusalem. They would have to abandon what they knew and head 700 miles west toward Jerusalem to fulfill the prophecy and God's calling. We can't forget that they had few memories, if any, of Jerusalem, which, by this time, was completely destroyed. Its walls, the homes, and the Temple had been reduced to little more than pieces and memories.

Today, God calls us to do the same. We need to let go of everything that has kept us from entering God's fullness and his calling for our lives. He is not content to leave us in a fallen state, but calls us to arise and ascend! This may mean we will have to go into unknown areas or face things we know very little about. God's main calling is for us to step out of our comfort zone and begin to stretch our faith.

If we want to experience revival, we must be willing to leave behind what we know and enter a more profound level of service and commitment with God. We must move in faith toward the unknown to accomplish what the Spirit of God wants. This can only happen when the Holy Ghost moves in our hearts.

> *"Then the family heads of Judah and Benjamin, and the priests and Levites--everyone whose heart God had moved —-prepared to go up and build the house of the LORD in Jerusalem. All their neighbors assisted them with articles of silver and gold, with goods and livestock, and with valuable gifts, in addition to all the freewill offerings." (Ezra 1:5-6)*

Please note that God had worked in their spirits. They received an awakening to leave what they knew and begin to do what God wanted for them. This same thing must happen with all of us if we wish to move in faith from the familiar to a new spiritual level.

When you study the journey in the book of Ezra, it describes the exiles who were moved by God to return to Jerusalem. You may be able to see yourself in any of these groups. It might just be that your heart is currently being stirred by the Holy Ghost. Perhaps you have felt a void in this season. You might have experienced joy but still feel as if something was missing. Maybe when you felt weak, you remembered the times when God was your everything. It might be a fact that you have spent so much time away from the church, far from God's presence, distant from the place where you found Jesus for the first time, that you lost all memory of your relationship with God.

The generation that responded to God's call to return to Judah consisted of those who were born into captivity because of their parents. They didn't choose to be born under those conditions; they simply were. This could be your current reality. You may possibly feel that what you have had to go through is unfair. It is something you did not deserve, and being far from God has blocked your knowledge of how to return. I want to remind you that God never gives up. From Genesis to the book of Revelation, the Bible shows us how he constantly tries to have an intimate relationship with us.

This call to arise and ascend to the altar is meant for everyone. Nevertheless, there is an urgency on those who have been called to leadership. The calling to rebuild the altar is for people who have fallen into a conformity that has prevented them from reaching new spiritual levels that God wishes them to discover. These are the same people who have drifted away from God for different reasons. They have abandoned their faith communities, their callings, and everything related to their relationship with God.

There are also many children whose parents decided to walk away from the Lord and, as a consequence, the generations that followed them have remained away as well. Many walked away from God during the pandemic, a very scary time in history. How tragic to think that they left God behind just when they needed His love and protection more than ever. Instead of running to the shelter of His arms, they stepped away from their callings and godly purpose. They have abandoned their ministries and are discouraged and frustrated.

It seems to me that most people are quick to blame God when something goes wrong, but slow to thank Him when He answers their prayers or blesses them in some way. Do you remember the story of the ten lepers Jesus healed? (The story is found in the 17th chapter of Luke.) Ten men were healed. But only one came back to thank Him. We are not so different from those nine ungrateful fellows. May the Lord open our eyes to the blessings He pours out on us, and fill our hearts with gratitude.

This is not just about ones who drifted away from a church or faith community; this calling is also for people who visit a Temple every week, but their hearts are far from God's presence. These are people who need to revive the gift of God in them. They are worshipers and servers who have converted a personal relationship with God into nothing more than a custom or habit.

Who were the exiled who decided to return, as stated in the second chapter of Ezra? The same people God is calling today. If you look up the definition of *exiled* in the dictionary, you will find something like (a person) *having been expelled and barred from one's native country*, typically for political or punitive reasons. Depending on the Bible version you read, they could have been described as extradited prisoners.

Now, the question is: where are you seeking refuge today? Why did you abandon your place? Regardless of why you drifted away from the presence of God or became discouraged, God is using this book like the decree he stirred in the heart of King Cyrus – to call your heart back to the altar. God wants to reinstate you, but you have to willingly accept this calling first.

The book of Ezra tells us that the people returning to Judah were the Israelites, their families, priests and religious leaders, Levites, singers, servants, men who worked in the house of the Lord, and the sons of Solomon's servants. They were a whole generation of servers who were far from their place of purpose. Can you identify with any of these people? From the heads of households to teachers, evangelists, worshipers, and people skilled in arts, God was calling them all to come home to Him.

The Holy Spirit yearns to revive the gift of God that lives within you. When God first created you, he instilled within you gifts that are in accordance with your earthly purpose and heavenly calling. This is why there are people who can play an instrument without ever receiving a formal class and others who can sing beautifully without any voice training. All around us are people who are gifted with their hands, their voices, and in other important ways, but many of them are lost and confused, far from the One Who promises, "Come to me, all of you who work and have heavy loads. I will give you rest." (Matthew 11:28)

We are all exiles

What does it feel like to be an exile? I believe it's something just about everyone has experienced at one time or another. Those of us who are believers know the feeling of being exiles here on earth. We know that our real home is in Heaven, and until we get there, most of us will feel a bit homesick and uneasy about much that takes place in the culture around us. One man said that he had always felt a tinge of sadness and longing for something, but he couldn't figure out what it was. Then one day it came to him that it was Heaven he was homesick for. He longed to meet the Lord face to face, and until that day came he would always feel the sadness that comes from separation.

I know hundreds of people who have come into the United States from foreign countries. Almost all of them came here to seek a better life for themselves and their children. They came to escape abject poverty and oppression, and they love America with a passion. And yet, they are exiles in many ways.

Many came here not knowing the language, or understanding the culture. They didn't know the little gestures that are expected in "polite" American society. Parents watched as their children struggled in school because they didn't know English. Some suffered at the hands of bullies and teachers who considered them to be dumb, rather than taking into consideration that they were new to the United States.

Am I painting a too-bleak picture? Of course, I'm talking about the worst case in all of these situations. Many immigrant families have been welcomed into their new neighborhood and schools with open arms. They have been given whatever help they needed to make the transition to life in America. But even in these situations, they are strangers in a strange land. Exiles.

Thousands of the brave American men and women who are serving on mission fields around the world also know what it's like to be exiles. Before they go off to the countries where they are going to serve God, they need to learn about the cultural taboos. For example, in some countries, reaching out to shake someone's hand is seen as aggressive, an invasion of the other person's personal space. In many other nations, hand gestures such as the okay sign, the peace sign or crossing your fingers are all considered to be vulgar. Oh, yes, and it is a terrible insult in Arabic countries to refuse food when it's offered. It doesn't matter if you've just had a filling meal, no excuses will be accepted.

One missionary was celebrated with a pig roast when he arrived in his new community in Central Africa. It was one of those occasions where the entire pig is roasted, as in a Hawaiian luau. Mmmmm! That roast pork sure smelled terrific.

But his hosts smiled and explained that they were bringing him something very special! He almost fainted when they honored him with a heaping platter of. . .pig intestines.

One country's treasure is another country's refuse.

Incidentally another man, who was on a mission trip to Mozambique said that his hosts asked him if Americans eat mice. When he answered that we don't, the host replied, "Oh, you should try them. They are delicious."

Before I leave this subject behind, I want to mention that you don't have to leave the United States to feel like an exile. There are so many different dialects, customs, and ways of phrasing things that it may be difficult for a person from New England to understand what is being said by someone from the deep South.

We are so different, but if we are believers, we are all one in Christ. The construction worker in New York is one with the professor in Louisiana, the professor in Louisiana is one with the surfer in Southern California, and the surfer in California is one with the nurse in the Bronx. There are so many differences between us, but we are one in Jesus!

As the Apostle Paul says:

> "Each of us is a part of the one body of Christ. Some of us are Jews, some are Gentiles, some are slaves, and some are free. But the Holy Spirit has fitted us all together into one body. We have been baptized into Christ's body by the one Spirit, and have all been given that same Holy Spirit." (1 Corinthians 12:13)

And again:

> There is no longer Jew or Gentile, slave or free, male and female. For you are all one in Christ Jesus. (Galatians 3:28)

There can be no doubt that there were a great many differences among the exiles who returned to Jerusalem under Ezra's leadership. Some were fresh-faced youngsters while others were bearded old men whose lined faces told of their long lives. Some had amassed great wealth in Babylonia, while others were just getting by. There were differences in educational status, marital status, etc. They were not at all the same, but they came together as one to rebuild their ancestral home despite the challenges and obstacles they faced.

As I said, we are all exiles and we are all different. But let us emulate the exiles of long ago and work together to build God's kingdom.

The story of Ezra is truly amazing. I can't think of any other example in all of history where a conquering king encouraged and allowed thousands of people, once regarded as enemies, to rebuild their vanquished nation. From a purely political point of view it doesn't make sense. Why allow your enemy to regain power and rekindle a sense of nationalism and patriotism in their land?

Jerusalem was rebuilt for the same reason it was destroyed—because God willed it. No king or other ruler on earth can ever stand against God or diminish the power of His Word. This makes me think about the condition of the Christian church in Russia and Eastern Europe. For about 70 years under communist rule, Christians were persecuted for their faith. People were not allowed to own Bibles. Telling someone about Christ was a serious crime. Some churches were padlocked. Others were used as museums. Many Christians were beaten, imprisoned and even executed for their faith. The Christian religion was ridiculed in schools. Children were told that hope for the future was found in the achievements of Soviet workers, scientists and soldiers; not in believing "ancient superstitions."

Communist leaders predicted again and again that Christianity would be completely dead in a few short years. So what happened? Communism has gone, but the church is stronger than ever. As soon as communist rule was overthrown in Europe, churches were jammed full of people, ecstatic that they were now free to openly worship God and share their faith. Thousands of seekers also came to church--some for the first time in their lives--because they wanted to learn about Jesus.

Seventy years under communism. Seventy years in exile in Babylonia. In both of these situations, Satan probably thought he was winning the battle for the minds and souls of men. But as he discovered, nothing can stop the Kingdom of God as it marches against the gates of hell.

Children of God without a home

Over the years I've run into homeless people on the street, and have asked them to share their stories. Some are obviously mentally ill and need to be in a shelter where someone can take care of them. But others seem bright and articulate. They once had solid, productive lives. They worked, paid their bills, and were contributing members of society.

Often, they tell me that they were once actively involved in a Christian community. How tragic that many who are singing on the streets today once sang at the altar for the honor of God. They once had wonderful gifts that they used for the glory of God and the building of His kingdom. Somewhere along their journey they lost their way and wandered out of the light and into the darkness.

It is never too late to return home to God. But sadly, some never make the decision to return to the faithful Shepherd who loves them so much He was willing to give His life for them.

Just the other day, someone sent me an article from the New York Times about a once-prominent man who lost his way on the streets of Bend, Oregon--a thriving community of about 100,000. His name was Craig Coyner, and he had once served as mayor of Bend. He had also been a powerful attorney who fought for the rights of people who were stuck in desperate poverty.

He had a wife and two children and owned his own home. But then, slowly at first but much rapidly later on, his life began to unravel. His marriage broke up, and after his ex-wife remarried, he lost contact with his daughters. He suffered from untreated mental illness and tried to cover his pain with alcohol, which only led him deeper into the darkness. Even then, he would often spend time at the Bend Community Center, helping serve meals to people who were down on their luck.

Reporter Mike Baker wrote, "Last fall, as overnight temperatures were dipping below 20 degrees, Frankie Smalley, a homeless friend, walked through town to track down Mr. Coyner. Then he came upon a yellow tent near Walmart. "Hey Craig, you in there' he called out.

He heard a voice inside and pulled back the tent flap. A pungent smell of urine and feces filled the air. Inside, Mr. Coyner's shoes were soaking wet, his feet so frostbitten he was hobbling with pain when he tried to stand up.

"He wound up at the hospital, where he was treated for frostbite, but he was soon discharged to the city's new low-barrier shelter. It had room for 100 but often had many more sleeping there.

"The frostbite had damaged Mr. Coyner's toes so badly that he had to go back to the hospital at the end of January for an amputation. There were complications. After the surgery, he had a stroke that left him unable to speak."

On February 14, Valentines Day, former Bend Mayor Craig Coyner passed away.

This is a tragic story that is often repeated in cities across America. Yet I believe that God does not want anyone to be lost and lonely, living alone in the midst of the bustling city. He longs for every hurting man, woman and child to come home to Him.

Lord, God, we are desperately in need of revival. The word *revival* is heard frequently in church, but it has been reduced to manifestations of the Holy Ghost or the visibility of certain gifts. The real revival referenced in the book of Ezra is the revival of the heart of God's children. That revival is reflected in true repentance, the conversion of the saints, visitation to the incarcerated, and attention to our seniors. All of this is also a sign of revival. Need is all around us, and those called to reconstruct should cover it.

The biggest evidence that proves we haven't answered God's call is the lack of bravery needed to confront the things that are happening within the church and around the world. We are not only indifferent to what is happening in front of our eyes, but we also have become so accustomed to these things that they no longer affect us. I believe many will agree that a big absence of sin conviction currently exists as well as a lack of fear and reverence of God.

There is very little astonishment regarding the lack of God in our society. Exposure to pornography has become common. There is no more desperation for the lost souls who are headed to hell. There is no sense of urgency to talk about Christ to others. There is a lot of indifference in teaching about what is infallible in the Bible and on the amount of time that we should devote to prayer with God. If people call us out on these things, we agree they are horrible, but then we turn over and continue sleeping.

What is coming next?

I truly believe that the next event in God's calendar is not the rapture of the church but the revival of His people before the return of Christ. The Father's biggest move on earth will be the awakening that will begin with the church that will--in turn--provoke millions of people to return to Christ. We need to turn back to God.

I recently heard how an evangelist shocked the congregation he was addressing by saying in his sermon, "I can see that nobody here really believes in hell."

What? This was a Bible-believing evangelical congregation. Yes, they believed in hell--and heaven, and salvation through faith in Jesus. What on earth was he talking about?

Then he went on to explain.

"If you really believed in hell, and thought it was a place of eternal punishment, you wouldn't be here tonight listening to me. You'd be out on the streets, grabbing people by their lapels and begging them to accept Jesus and avoid the excruciating pain of hell."

Some people were offended. But others understood. Hell is real. There is only one way to escape the agony of its flames and that is through faith in Jesus Christ. All around us are souls that are bound for the flames, unless we can convince them to come back home to the altar of God!

Overthrow the giants

I can't close this chapter without bringing to your attention how the second chapter of Ezra concludes: "When they arrived at the Temple of the LORD in Jerusalem, some of the family leaders made voluntary offerings toward the rebuilding of God's Temple on its original site, and each leader gave as much as he could"(Ezra 2:68-69).

This group that accepted the calling and obeyed the voice of the Father had come to rebuild the altar at the same place it had been destroyed. Many times we abandon situations, step out of the lives of people, leave giants without overthrowing them, end up at the same place, and have to face what we should have never abandoned, pushed aside, denied, or ignored. The giant that you don't overthrow will come back to haunt you.

Sometimes, in order to move forward, we need to step backward. God is a sovereign God, and He could have easily ordered a new Temple and a new altar to be built in any place, but that wasn't the case. God took them to the ruins, to the abandoned and deserted place, where it probably looked dirty, and forgotten. In that same forsaken place of ruins, a safe place would be lifted, a place where the Father would restore His relationship with His people. The abandoned place would be the encounter for true liberty to regain joy and what was ruined to be restored.

No matter what your condition may be today, even if you feel you are not worthy of reclaiming your godly calling, Jesus says to you, *"He who comes to me I will never cast out."* (John 6:37, Modern English Version) Mankind will always be more severe on other people than God will ever be. That is why King David said: "Let us fall into the hands of the LORD, for his mercy is great. Do not let me fall into human hands." (2 Samuel 24:14). If you start to understand the calling and path toward a revival in the book of Ezra, you will get what the Holy Spirit wants to speak into your heart.

God started the revival by stirring the heart of an ungodly man--but a man in a position of power who would allow His people to return to the place from which they should have never been cast out. Afterward, He called into willing hearts of His children so that they themselves yearned to return and regain a relationship with God. We can see that even though the calling is available for everyone, there are many who refuse it, to their own detriment.

We can also see that God wishes to give you victory in the same scenario in which you received defeat. It's my heart's desire that as you continue to read the following chapters, God's calling on your life will become more persistent. God moved my heart to write this book that now becomes His decree, calling you to rebuild your altar. As you will see, I am not referring to a physical structure, but rather, His presence in your life.

Lesson #4 from the Book of Ezra

Imagine how Ezra must have felt when he first heard that thousands of Jews were going back to Jerusalem to undo the damage that had befallen the great city. He now knew for certain that all things are indeed possible with God. Ezra loved Jerusalem with a passion, even though he had never been there. Wouldn't it be wonderful if all believers today felt the same way about Heaven? Heaven is our true home and we must never lose sight of that. Are you homesick for Heaven? I am! And I will do everything I can to take as many people as possible with me when I go.

QUESTIONS FOR SPIRITUAL REFLECTION

1. Have you comprehended the calling over your life to collaborate with the kingdom in favor of God's children?

2. Have you meditated on who around you today needs to know God or reconcile their lives with Him?

3. Do you have a talent or gift from God that you have stopped using? What will you do to revitalize the use of this precious gift?

____

____

____

4. Who walks by you each day? Do they inspire and motivate you to move closer to God?

____

____

____

5

RESTORING THE RUINS

Then Jeshua son of Jehozadak joined his fellow priests and Zerubbabel son of Shealtiel with his family in rebuilding the altar of the God of Israel. They wanted to sacrifice burnt offerings on it, as instructed in the Law of Moses, the man of God (Ezra 3:2).

WHEN GOD CALLED THE ISRAELITES TO RETURN to Judah from Babylonia, they were not going home. Far from it. Entire generations had grown up in exile. They had not spent a single moment of their lives in "the Promised Land." Judah had an important place in their hearts because it was the land their grandparents and great grandparents had once called home, but it was more of a fantasy to them than a tangible reality.

Think of what it would be like if all the people who came to the United States from other countries were suddenly told that they could all go back "home." How many of them would want to go? Very few, I imagine. Although they are proud of their heritage as Mexicans, Haitians, Europeans, Africans, Asians, and so on, they consider themselves to be Americans first.

Yes, it was a challenge for the Jews of Babylon to agree to give up everything they owned and move toward the unknown. It took bravery to set aside fear and uncertainty--to pack up their belongings and move to a country that many had not even seen before. Let's take a closer look at some of the challenges they had to face.

First of all, the land they had to cross to get back to Judah was full of dangers. Much of the land was desert, which meant that water was scarce and temperatures could reach well over 100 degrees in the middle of the day. There were also many wild animals roaming through the Middle East in those days – lions, jackals and poisonous snakes of all kinds. Another serious threat came from bands of robbers who had absolutely no regard for human life.

The Bible says that it took four months for Ezra and the people who accompanied him to make the journey from Babylon to Jerusalem. The trip was a difficult one and could have been deadly for young children and the elderly. But Ezra writes: *"We broke camp at the Ahava Canal on April 19 and started off to Jerusalem. And the gracious hand of our God protected us and saved us from enemies and bandits along the way."* (Ezra 8:31)

It would be correct to say that many of the children of Israel risked their lives by obeying God's call to come "home." But even through dangerous and unknown ways, Jehovah was with them. None of them were harmed because when you walk in obedience, God's protection is all over you. As David wrote in Psalm 23:4:

> ***"Even when I walk***
> ***through the darkest valley,***
> ***I will not be afraid,***
> ***for you are close beside me.***
> ***Your rod and your staff***
> ***protect and comfort me."***

The Bible tells us that God is always ready to welcome the sinner who returns to the fold. He is the Good Shepherd who is willing to sacrifice His life to rescue his sheep from danger. (John 10:11) In His Parable of the Prodigal Son, Jesus paints a picture of God running out to meet the one who is returning home from a life of sin and debauchery:

> *And while he was still a long way off, his father saw him coming. Filled with love and compassion, he ran to his son, embraced him, and kissed him. His son said to him, "Father, I have*

*sinned against both heaven and you, and I am
no longer worthy of being called your son."*

*But his father said to the servants, "Quick!
Bring the finest robe in the house and put it
on him. Get a ring for his finger and sandals
for his feet. And kill the calf we have been fat-
tening. We must celebrate with a feast, for this
son of mine was dead and has now returned to
life. He was lost, but now he is found." So the
party began (Luke 15:20-24).*

Even though this is the case, it is also true that when
a child of God decides to come back to the Father, the
path will not always be easy. There are those who are
still trapped in a life of sin, and feel that their former
"partner in crime" is turning his or her back on them.
They are doing their best to get their old friend to rejoin
them in their life of drinking, drugs, sexual perversion
or whatever it is that has them bound. Satan is also there,
whispering in their ear, "Don't you remember how much
fun we had?"

Nevertheless, nothing can compare to the joy of
knowing that you are walking in obedience and have
God's favor.

The Bible often speaks about God's coverage over us.
Isaiah 54:15 says: "If any nation comes to fight you, it is
not because I sent them. Whoever attacks you will go

down in defeat." In addition, Deuteronomy 28:7 says: *"The LORD will conquer your enemies when they attack you. They will attack you from one direction, but they will scatter from you in seven!"* God has promised to give protection to His children. Having said this, fear should not detain you from accepting God's calling nor cause you to stop the works that need to be accomplished.

Just as God protected all those who made the journey back to Judah to help rebuild the Temple, He will guard you from danger on your own journey back to Him. Even if you are walking into the unknown, toward a place you have never been before, regardless of the uncertainty, if you are responding to God's calling, He will protect you.

The children of God finally arrived at Jerusalem, in the territory of Judah, and settled in. This is when the most beautiful phase of the book of Ezra begins--the reconstruction of God's house.

The Holy Spirit appointed leaders among the children of God so that they would be guided throughout this whole process. God is always seeking those who can lead His people. This is one of the dire needs many churches are facing today--the lack of leadership. That is why the first hearts the Lord is stirring are the hearts of the leaders appointed for this time.

In 2018, we began a construction project in the church we had been leading for twenty years. We wanted to rebuild the altar in the Temple, and I remember vividly the amount of sacrifice that was required for a project like this.

Often, before you can rebuild, you have to tear down. In other words, before you can build a new altar, you must demolish the strongholds in your life. The apostle Paul says in 2 Corinthians 10:4-5, *"We use God's mighty weapons, not worldly weapons, to knock down the strongholds of human reasoning and to destroy false arguments." The altar call is a calling to use those gifts that can "destroy every proud obstacle that keeps people from knowing God. We capture their rebellious thoughts and teach them to obey Christ."*

The process that the children of God began had a double purpose: 1) rebuild the Temple that had been destroyed and 2)remember the circumstances of past events. They needed to know their true story, their real cause, and why their parents wound up spending seventy years in captivity. When we begin to revive God's purpose in our lives, some things will be done in our earthly experience and others in the spiritual realm.

The people who started the work in Jerusalem were scared. They were afraid of the hostile people who surrounded them--people who had no desire to see the Jewish nation rise from the ashes. Even so, they did not let fear keep them from doing what God had told them to do. They were determined to follow the Word of the Lord no matter what. This is precisely the determination we must have when we decide to restore our relationship with the Lord.

It's almost always true that the first people who become obstacles to you when you are trying to get closer to God are your closest friends and family. Some of these people may have even blamed you for keeping them from getting closer to God. They couldn't attend church regularly because you didn't want them to go. They could give as God commands us to because they were afraid you would be angry.

But then your attitude changed. All of a sudden you wanted to be in church every time the doors were open. You suddenly cared about the Lord's work all around the world and wanted to give liberally to support the kingdom. But it was apparent that the people who had always blamed you for holding them back didn't really want to do move forward. They were using your "bad" behavior as an excuse, although they didn't even know it.

I'm not saying that the situation I've just described is always the case. Most Christian families are filled with joy when their straying loved one returns to the altar. But I've seen enough to know that this is not always the case.

In fact, I wonder if some of Ezra's friends might have been whispering in his ear, "What are you thinking, bro? You don't want to go back to Jerusalem. I've heard the place is a mess. They don't have all the modern conveniences we have here in Babylonia. And besides, there's a lot of unsavory types hanging around there."

I don't know if anybody spoke to Ezra like that, but I wouldn't be surprised. And, to his credit, if they did, he didn't listen to them. Neither should we listen to those who have reasons why we shouldn't get too close to God.

A very important detail we observe during this phase of the reconstruction of the Temple is that the Jews had resumed offering sacrifices and hosting the traditional ceremonies that had been established by God.

Don't sell yourself short

Too often, when we receive a godly calling, we minimize our ability and sell ourselves short. Don't get me wrong. Of course, there are things we need to organize and modify when we are serving the Lord--but we often tend to go overboard with excuses. It happened with Moses when God called him to be the deliverer of His people. He actually gave God five reasons why he didn't want to answer the calling.

Excuse Number One: *"But Moses protested to God, 'Who am I to appear before Pharaoh? Who am I to lead the people of Israel out of Egypt?'"* (Exodus 3:11) This excuse was mainly due to the fact that he had been working as a shepherd for over twenty years, and this profession was despised by the Egyptians. Moses felt unworthy.

Excuse Number Two: *"But Moses protested, 'If I go to the people of Israel and tell them, "The God of your ancestors has sent me to you," they will ask me, "What is his name?" Then what should I tell them?'" (Exodus 3:13).* Moses was afraid of his credibility in the eyes of the people of Israel.

Excuse Number Three: *"Then Moses answered, 'What if they won't believe me or listen to me?'"* (Exodus 4:1). He not only doubted his credibility, but his leadership and influence as well.

Excuse Number Four: Moses, pleaded, *"O Lord, I'm not very good with words. I never have been, and I'm not now, even though You have spoken to me. I get tongue-tied, and my words get tangled" (Exodus 4:10).* When God looked at Moses, He did not see any weakness in him that could prevent him from fulfilling his calling. It was Moses himself who tried to use his incapacity as an excuse.

Excuse Number Five: "But Moses again pleaded, 'Lord, please! Send anyone else'" (Exodus 4:13). In other words, give this assignment to the person who could truly do the job. Many times we act like Moses: we believe we cannot do the things God has called us to do, doubt our abilities and the grace that God has given us, diminish ourselves, use our weaknesses against ourselves, and believe there are people better able to do the work than us.

For every excuse Moses tried to use, God had a counter answer and a solution. God doesn't make mistakes. If He has placed a concern in your heart, it's because you can handle the calling. This is about being obedient while you walk. It's about worshiping the Father while you heal.

The children of Israel began to offer sacrifices and celebrate the traditional feasts despite the Temple not being rebuilt yet. Salvation is granted instantly when we surrender to Jesus, but sanctification is a daily process until His return. God is calling you to the Altar, to the place of His presence. He is aware of your sins, weaknesses, and trials, and He still wants to heal, restore, and reinstate you.

Asking for Help Is Part of the Process

When the reconstruction of Jerusalem finally started, carpenters and stonemasons were hired to help in the work that was taking place. The task ahead of them would not be easy. It was a process that would take time and have to be done in phases.

When something is built for the first time, you have total control of how everything is done. This includes the materials used and the final design. When you have a remodeling project, you don't necessarily have all of the information you wished you had. You don't know the materials that were used or might not have the original design at hand nor the awareness of what is salvageable from the original construction.

The same happens with us when we withdraw from God's presence. When God first created us, we were perfect. He knew how He would create us, the gifts and talents He would bestow upon us, and He placed within us a purpose and destiny.

Tragically, many have abandoned their purpose and destiny, extinguished the fire that was burning on the altar and run away from God. They feel that their lives have been reduced to ruins because of the strong trials they have faced, and they feel that they need a do-over – but they don't know how to find a new start.

Starting over is not easy – but if we seek help, allow ourselves to be vulnerable and set aside our pride, we can do it the same way the people who returned to Judah did. They were aware they needed help, they requested it, and they received it.

Many children of God don't receive the healing they need or achieve reconciliation with the Father simply due to pride. This is not about being self-sufficient. In fact, the Word of God says in 1 Corinthians 10:12: "If you think you are standing strong, be careful not to fall." We need to be humble enough to understand when we are in the wrong and need someone to walk by our side and help us find our way back to Christ.

God built us so that we need the support and help of other people. His Father's heart was broken when he saw

Adam all by himself in the Garden of Eden. He said: "*It is not good for the man to be alone. I will make a helper who is just right for him*" (*Genesis 2:18*). When we read the Bible's account of the Great Flood, we find that God saved sets of partners--Noah and his wife, and Noah's three sons and their wives. Even the animals were saved in pairs of males and females. Part of this was to ensure the continuation of each species after the flood, but I also think it was a symbol of God's understanding that we all need the companionship and support of other human beings.

I love these words from the book of Ecclesiastes:

> *Two people are better off than one, for they can help each other succeed. If one person falls, the other can reach out and help. But someone who falls alone is in real trouble. Likewise, two people lying close together can keep each other warm. But how can one be warm alone? A person standing alone can be attacked and defeated, but two can stand back-to-back and conquer. Three are even better, for a triple-braided cord is not easily broken (Ecclesiastes 4:9-12).*

If you are seeking to rebuild your relationship with God, you are likely to need the help of your brothers and sisters in Christ. You will also need the understanding and assistance of your friends, your family members, plus the pastors, elders and other leaders of your church.

You will especially need the help of people who have wisdom in the areas of your biggest weaknesses.

As the book of Proverbs tells us: "Plans go wrong for lack of advice; many advisers bring success" (Proverbs 15:22).

In Search of a New Generation

Something beautiful happened during the reconstruction of the Temple under the leadership of Zerubbabel and Jeshua. They decided to appoint young Levites as leaders in the reconstruction of God's Temple:

> *"The construction of the Temple of God began in midspring, during the second year after they arrived in Jerusalem. The work force was made up of everyone who had returned from exile, including Zerubbabel son of Shealtiel, Jeshua son of Jehozadak and his fellow priests, and all the Levites. The Levites who were twenty years old or older were put in charge of rebuilding the LORD's Temple" (Ezra 3:8).*

Don't ever think that God can't use you because you are too young (or too old, for that matter). Some of the Levites who were working on rebuilding the Temple were barely out of their teens.

Remember that David was just a boy when he went out to do battle against the Philistine giant, Goliath. When Samuel came to the house of Jesse to anoint the next king of Israel, Jesse didn't even think to bring his youngest son out to see the prophet. Why? Again, because David was just a kid. He probably wasn't even shaving yet. Surely, he couldn't be the one Samuel was seeking. But guess what? Man looks at the outside of a person, but God looks on the heart.

As Paul wrote to Timothy: *"Don't let anyone think less of you because you are young. Be an example to all believers in what you say, in the way you live, in your love, your faith, and your purity"* (1 Timothy 4:12).

Despite these and other examples throughout the Bible which show us that age doesn't really matter to God, most of us tend to minimize ourselves when we compare ourselves to those who have been doing the works of God longer than we have. The truth is that the calling to be in God's presence and have a relationship with Him is for everyone. It doesn't matter how long you have known the Lord or confessed Him; God wants you to arrive at the safe and secrete place so that you can worship Him.

As I look around, I can see that God is lifting up a new generation so they can become leaders in our faith communities. One of the areas of weakness I continue to see in our faith-based communities is the lack of youth in leadership positions--especially in the five ministries

Jesus established: Apostles, prophets, pastors, teachers, and evangelists. We need to understand that God is calling all generations to the altar, from the youngest to the oldest.

Did you know that Billy Graham was just 28 years old when he held his first crusade, bringing 6,000 people together to hear the gospel in Grand Rapids, Michigan?

How about Oral Roberts? He was 30 when he began his itinerant healing ministry and 45 when he founded Oral Roberts University.

And Joel Osteen was 36 when he became lead pastor of Lakewood Church in Houston.

These are just three examples, basically off the top of my head. There are many others I could name. Jesus Himself had only been in His human body for 33 years when He was crucified. His earthly ministry lasted just three years, beginning was He was only 30.

And then there was a boy named Josiah. You can find his story beginning in the 34th chapter of 2 Chronicles:

> *Josiah was eight years old when he became king, and he reigned in Jerusalem thirty-one years. He did what was pleasing in the LORD's sight and followed the example of his ancestor*

David. He did not turn away from doing what was right.

During the eighth year of his reign, while he was still young, Josiah began to seek the God of his ancestor David. Then in the twelfth year he began to purify Judah and Jerusalem, destroying all the pagan shrines, the Asherah poles, and the carved idols and cast images. He ordered that the altars of Baal be demolished and that the incense altars which stood above them be broken down. He also made sure that the Asherah poles, the carved idols, and the cast images were smashed and scattered over the graves of those who had sacrificed to them. He burned the bones of the pagan priests on their own altars, and so he purified Judah and Jerusalem.

He did the same thing in the towns of Manasseh, Ephraim, and Simeon, even as far as Naphtali, and in the regions all around them. He destroyed the pagan altars and the Asherah poles, and he crushed the idols into dust. He cut down all the incense altars throughout the land of Israel. Finally, he returned to Jerusalem (2 Chronicles 34:1-7).

What an amazing legacy for a young man who was only eight years old when he first ascended to the throne. Don't ever think that you can't serve the Lord because you are too young, or too old, or too average. No matter who you are. No matter your station in life. God can and will use you if you let Him.

Unfortunately, a lot of older people get impatient with kids. They get on our nerves because they're so noisy. They may spill things on the brand-new carpets. They don't always watch where they're going, which can be really aggravating as you're leaving the sanctuary after the Sunday morning service. They may whisper and giggle when they should be paying attention to the sermon. And, let's face it, it can be pretty hard to deal with the weird way teenagers dress. (Why can't they behave like normal people?)

I hope you understand that I'm saying all this with a smile on my face, because I understand that today's children are our leaders of tomorrow – and tomorrow will be here before we know it. If the young people in your church get on your nerves, the best thing you can do is pray for patience. Ask the Lord to help you remember what your life was like when you were young – when you may have talked too loud, not paid attention to where you were going, etc. Ask Him to help you love the young men and women in your church and encourage them in their faith walk. You can build lasting faith in these kids by letting them know that you care about them and want to see them blessed by God. You can help them think of the church as a happy place so they will continue to attend when they are older. I guarantee you, your words of encouragement will have a lasting positive effect on a young man or woman. Criticize sparingly, encourage generously. Make it a habit to pray that God will use you to build up and encourage in every encounter, and never to tear down or destroy.

You may even feel God leading you to teach Sunday school. In my own life, I remember the men and women--some of them quite old, or so I thought, who taught me about Jesus. They encouraged me to memorize Bible verses such as John 3:16, the 23rd Psalm and The Lord's Prayer. And they blessed me whenever they could. It was largely because of their love and kindness that I was able to hear and respond to God's call into the ministry.

You may never find out, until you get to Heaven, how many people have come into the kingdom because you touched a young person with the love of Christ.

Better opportunities

The youth who serve the Lord today have a better opportunity to reach others since they were born into the era of technology. The concept of "Go into all the world and preach the Good News to everyone" (Mark 16:15) is as easy as doing a live transmission on social media, and within seconds, the life-changing message can be heard anywhere in the world. Because of social media, today's youth have the ability to communicate their message in a language their generation understands.

I am always amazed how today's people understand modern technology. Those of us who are a little bit older may struggle with some of the ins and outs of computer technology. But whenever I run into trouble, I simply ask one of my kids and they will bail me out. Not only that, but sometimes after I've struggled with some problem for an hour or more, they will clean it up for me in a couple of minutes. I believe this technological know-how is a gift from God to help spread the message of Christ's love into all the world – which the Bible says will happen before He returns.

The reality is that the world's population is growing older, and there are fewer births each year. Our youth are very important to God's plans for the last days as described in Acts 2:17:

"In the last days,' God says, 'I will pour out my Spirit upon all people. Your sons and daughters will prophesy. Your young men will see visions, and your old men will dream dreams."

Living on past glories

After seventy years of captivity, the children of God were able to go back to the Promised Land. They not only were living in Jerusalem but were also seeing the glory of God's temple revived. The third chapter of the book of Ezra tells of a very special achievement.

When the builders completed the foundation of the LORD's Temple, the priests put on their robes and took their places to blow their trumpets. And the Levites, descendants of Asaph, clashed their cymbals to praise the LORD, just as King David had prescribed. With praise and thanks, they sang this song to the LORD:

"He is so good! His faithful love for Israel endures forever!"

Then all the people gave a great shout, praising the LORD because the foundation of the LORD's Temple had been laid (Ezra 3:10-11).

The Word describes a scene in which some were singing worship songs; there was praise, and God's people were shouting that God was good. Nevertheless, while this victory was being celebrated, some people weren't able to join the celebration because they were trapped in past glories. Ezra 3:12-13 says:

But many of the older priests and Levites and family heads, who had seen the former Temple, wept aloud when they saw the foundation of this Temple being laid, while many others shouted for joy. No one could distinguish the sound of the shouts of joy from the sound of weeping, because the people made so much noise. And the sound was heard far away.

Remembering past glories and reminiscing about what God has done in our lives is not a bad thing. But when these memories prevent us from enjoying the present moment, we need to evaluate where our hearts are.

Many people are trapped in the past, thinking about past victories or brooding over mistakes they made or sins they committed long ago. If our sins have been washed away by the blood of Jesus and we are still brooding about them, I believe we are showing a lack of faith in the efficacy of Christ's sacrifice on our behalf. If Jesus tells us our sins have been forgiven, then why do we want to hold onto them and continue to punish ourselves for committing them? Yes, we need to be genuinely sorry for what we have done and ask God for forgiveness in Jesus' name. We must also repent of our sinful ways, which means that with God's help, we will never go there again. And once that has been done, we let them go.

People who live in the past often become trapped in the pain and dysfunction of yesterday. They simply don't know how to manage happiness and the new things God wants to give them. Letting go and healing from the past is in part one of the crucial things we must do when we answer God's calling.

For example, many of God's children have stayed away from the church because someone there hurt them, and they haven't healed. Some people have gone through losses that took away their desire to live. Others have suffered so greatly in their romantic relationships that they have decided to close themselves off and never love again.

There are many other examples of how living in the past will prevent you from enjoying the present and strip away your hope and expectations for the future. To be at God's altar means to be in His presence. It is in His presence that all soul wounds heal.

This is where you can find the peace that your heart desires. Responding to the calling of God involves going to the place of ruins, surrendering your losses to God, and allowing Him to rebuild and restore you so you can discover that your biggest glory is not in your past but your future. Paul wrote in Philippians 3:12:

> *I don't mean to say that I have already achieved these things or that I have already reached perfection. But I press on to possess that perfection for which Christ Jesus first possessed me.*

If, for any reason, you haven't advanced in your Christian walk, you must evaluate your life to see if you have been trapped in past glories that are preventing you from moving forward. You must become the living sacrifice on the altar and allow God to consume you. God wishes to restore you and give you joy and happiness, but it is important that you answer the calling and come to the Altar.

Lesson #5 from the Book of Ezra

After 70 long years away from their homeland, the Jewish people once again began making sacrifices on the newly rebuilt altar in Jerusalem. Can't you just imagine their joy as the new temple rose up before them. Finally, the people found their spiritual purpose again. Do you ever feel that you have lost something since you first accepted Christ and received the gift of the Holy Spirit? If so, it's time to return to the cross and ask Him to rekindle the fire of faith in you. Remember what Jesus said to the church at Smyrna: "But I have this complaint against you. You don't love me or each other as you did at first! Turn back to me and do the works you did at first" (Revelation 2:4-5).

QUESTIONS FOR
SPIRITUAL REFLECTION

1. Are there areas of your spiritual life that need to be restored? Can you name them?

\
\
\

2. How would you describe the restoration process in your life?

\
\
\

3. What have you had to let go of to enter God's process?

\
\
\

4. We know that salvation is instantaneous, but sanctification is a daily process. What does this process look like in your life?

____

____

____

5. How many times have you been held back from moving forward in your walk with Jesus because you are detained by the hurts or sins of the past or focused on the glories of the past?

____

____

____

6

OVERCOMING OBSTACLES AND WINNING BATTLES

*"The enemies of Judah and Benjamin heard that the exiles were rebuilding a Temple to the L*ord*, the God of Israel. So they approached Zerubbabel and the other leaders and said, 'Let us build with you, for we worship your God just as you do. We have sacrificed to him ever since King Esarhaddon of Assyria brought us here.' But Zerubbabel, Jeshua, and the other leaders of Israel replied, 'You may have no part in this work. We alone will build the Temple for the L*ord*, the God of Israel, just as King Cyrus of Persia commanded us.'"*
(Ezra 4:1-2)

In every war, there are two sides. In the spiritual world, it's the same. On one side, you have God the Father, Who is always seeking to have a relationship with humankind, and on the other side, you have Satan, who is determined to do whatever he can to disrupt the relationship between God and the beings He created. Whenever a purpose exists, there will always be opposition, and the Children of Israel were not exempt from this. When you read the fourth chapter of Ezra, you will see the great opposition they faced as they sought to rebuild the Temple that had been the centerpiece of Judah, and a beacon of the light of God's love for hundreds of years.

God's people have always had enemies. Throughout their history, entire nations have risen up against them again and again. Nevertheless, God has always defended His people and brought them through. Just look at the opposition Jesus experienced in his ministry as he prepared to fulfill his main purpose, which was to redeem all of humanity. Although He had done nothing wrong, He was whipped and beaten almost to death, and then murdered by being nailed to a wooden cross.

Even Jesus was tempted

When Jesus was in the desert after His baptism, the devil did everything he possibly could to prevent Him from fulfilling the mission His heavenly Father had given Him. For this reason, it shouldn't surprise us to read that not everyone was content to see the Jewish people back in the land of their ancestors. The same thing occurs in our lives whenever we make the decision to return to God, fix our lives, and follow the correct path. Satan is standing in our way shouting, "Oh no you don't!" But the devil is not the only one who tries to stop us. Look at what happened to Ezra and the others who had come back home from Babylonia:

> *The enemies of Judah and Benjamin heard that the exiles were rebuilding a Temple to the* LORD, *the God of Israel. So they approached Zerubbabel and the other leaders and said, "Let us build with you, for we worship your God just as you do. We have sacrificed to him ever since King Esarhaddon of Assyria brought us here."*
>
> *But Zerubbabel, Jeshua, and the other leaders of Israel replied, "You may have no part in this work. We alone will build the Temple for the* LORD, *the God of Israel, just as King Cyrus of Persia commanded us."*
>
> *Then the local residents tried to discourage and frighten the people of Judah to keep them from their work. They bribed agents to work against them and to frustrate their plans. This went on during the entire reign of King Cyrus of Persia and lasted until King Darius of Persia took the throne" (Ezra 4:1-5).*

There are several important details here we need to consider regarding the first opposition. The first is that the attack and anger came from people who presented themselves as believers and followers of the true God. At times the first attack we receive will come from people who confess to have God's love in their hearts, but their fruits and actions testify to something completely different.

As I mentioned earlier, when we decide to give our lives to Christ, those who are closest to us will often be the first to criticize us. This generally happens because they are closest to us, and thus are well acquainted with our weaknesses. The enemy knows that opposition from people who are not dear and near to our hearts doesn't have the same effect as criticism from those who are close to us.

These objectors initially wanted to be involved in the reconstruction of the Temple. They felt that because they had been in the territory for such a long time, it was their right to take part in such an important assignment. In fact, they highlighted the fact that they had been sacrificing offerings to the God of Israel since the moment they were established there and up to the moment that these exiles returned. So when they were not included, they were the first to oppose the entire project.

This portion of the story was not placed in the book of Ezra by chance. Rather, it's here to remind us that God always knows who our enemies are, and He also knows the tactics they will use to try to make us fall. God is never taken by surprise.

Perhaps you're going through something similar as you try to get up from the place where the enemy made you fall. It could be that some of your fellow believers have united with people in authority to come against you.

In this case, those opposed to the work of the exiles finally achieved their goal by writing a letter to King Artaxerxes, claiming that a rebuilt Jerusalem could lead to a rebellion against him. The Bible says that the king responded like this:

> *"The letter you sent has been translated and read to me. I ordered a search of the records and have found that Jerusalem has indeed been a hotbed of insurrection against many kings. In fact, rebellion and revolt are normal there! Powerful kings have ruled over Jerusalem and the entire province west of the Euphrates River, receiving tribute, customs, and tolls. Therefore, issue orders to have these men stop their work. That city must not be rebuilt except at my express command. Be diligent, and don't neglect this matter, for we must not permit the situation to harm the king's interests." (Ezra 4:18-22)*

The Bible goes on to say:

"When this letter from King Artaxerxes was read to Rehum, Shimshai, and their colleagues, they hurried to Jerusalem. Then, with a show of strength, they forced the Jews to stop building." (Ezra 4:23)

For more than two years, the Israelites had remained still without fulfilling the assignment God gave them. I have seen similar situations in our own day, when people are held back by criticism and challenges leveled by other "believers." Some have abandoned the faith community, others walked away from ministry, and some cut off all communication with God.

The reasons are many. Every person has their own "why." When you talk to them, you'll find that they can explain and justify their reasons. But even though their reasons might be valid--and no one minimizes what they are going through--it's not God's will for anyone to remain stuck in captivity.

We are called to reignite the works of God in our lives--to repair and rebuild His altar within us. Understand that I am not referring to a physical structure, but rather to the transformation of our hearts and minds in order to live a life of obedience to the Father.

Have you ever stopped God's work in your life because of fear, oppression, or internal and external pressures? Have you diminished the fire of the altar that burned in your heart and allowed a close relationship with the Lord to fall apart? In such desperate times, God will send godly men and women to us to speak on behalf of the kingdom and remind us that the works He has ordained must continue. God has promised to be with you until the end, and He always keeps His promises.

But as Paul writes in 2 Corinthians 6:14-16:

> *"Don't team up with those who are unbelievers. How can righteousness be a partner with wickedness? How can light live with darkness? What harmony can there be between Christ and the devil? How can a believer be a partner with an unbeliever? And what union can there be between God's Temple and idols? For we are the Temple of the living God."*

In the letter to the church at Ephesus, recorded in the second chapter of Revelation, Jesus praises the Ephesians because *"I know all the things you do. I have seen your hard work and your patient endurance. I know you don't tolerate evil people. You have examined the claims of those who say they are apostles but are not. You have discovered they are liars"* (Revelation 2:2).

Then, to the Church at Smyrna, He writes: *I know the blasphemy of those opposing you. They say they are Jews, but they are not, because their synagogue belongs to Satan"* (Revelation 2:9).

In both of these instances, people were seeking to sow discord among the brethren by claiming to be what they were not. In the first instance, they claimed to be apostles. In the second instance, they claimed to be faithful Jews, even though they had turned away from God. In the same way, there are imposters and phonies among us today, and we cannot allow them to cause us to take our eyes off the assignment God has given us. As Jesus says in Matthew 7:15-19:

> *"Beware of false prophets who come disguised as harmless sheep but are really vicious wolves. You can identify them by their fruit, that is, by the way they act. Can you pick grapes from thorn-bushes, or figs from thistles? A good tree produces good fruit, and a bad tree produces bad fruit. A good tree can't produce bad fruit, and a bad tree can't produce good fruit. So every tree that does not produce good fruit is chopped down and thrown into the fire. Yes, just as you can identify a tree by its fruit, so you can identify people by their actions.*

Please don't think I'm suggesting we need to become vigilantes, constantly checking to see that everyone else believes all the same things we do, and taking action against them when they don't. There are essentials, of course, such as believing that Jesus is the Son of God who died for our sins. But there are areas where we may disagree, such as when the Rapture will take place. As

St. Augustine said, "In essentials, unity. In non-essentials liberty. In all things, love."

And perhaps you have heard it said that a church is a hospital for sinners, not a museum for saints. We are imperfect and we are bound to have our differences.

But when we see some who are constantly sewing discord, or who are spreading doctrines that will lead people away from the doctrines that are found in the New Testament, then we must take action.

Churches are closing

According to an organization called Lifeway Research, more than 4,500 Protestant Churches across the United States closed their doors in 2019[10] – the last year   for   which   complete statistic are available. In the same year, an estimated 3,000 churches opened their doors for the first time. Do the math, and you will see that this leads to a net loss of 1,500 churches in one year! I have heard many reports of churches that were struggling to keep their doors open after fights over doctrine brought about splits, or caused membership to decline dramatically. It is clear to me that most, if not all, of these fights over doctrine were stirred up by Satan, who loves it when churches close down. (Of course, Satan uses human beings to carry out his plans.)

---

[10] Research.lifeway.com, "When One Church Door Closes, June 11, 2021

How can we change this sad situation, and continue to grow the church as Christ commands.

1) We can follow the advice of St. Augustine and practice unity in essentials, liberty in non-essentials, and love in all things.

2) When we see people in the church who are argumentative and divisive, we must take action against them, in love.

3) When false doctrine is being taught, or spread in any other way, we must come against it.

4) We must not be unequally yoked with unbelievers.

Lesson #6 from the Book of Ezra

"It's not over 'til it's over." That saying is attributed to the late Yankees Catcher Yogi Berra. He said it one year when the Yankees were "hopelessly" behind in the race for the American League pennant. And guess what. The Yankees came back and won everything. Every Christian should remember that it's not over until it's over. We serve a God who delights in snatching victory out of the jaws of defeat. That's one thing Ezra discovered after opponents of the Jews convinced King Artaxerxes that the rebuilding of Jerusalem must stop. The situation looked hopeless, but not for God. Artaxerxes died. Darius came to the throne – and ordered the work to go forward. What had seemed like the end was only a temporary break. Always remember it's not over until God says it's over.

QUESTIONS FOR SPIRITUAL REFLECTION

---

1. Did you face opposition when you decided to give your life to Christ? Explain.

____

____

____

2. Did any of that opposition come from unexpected sources? Explain your answer.

____

____

____

3. Name the enemy or enemies who have given you your toughest spiritual battles.

____

____

____

4. Tell of a time in your life when you your oppressors
    kept you from moving forward.

____

____

____

5. What tactics do you use to overcome your enemies?
    (For example: Prayer, the Word, Praise, etc.)

____

____

____

7

BY MY SPIRIT
SAYS THE LORD

At that time the prophets Haggai and Zechariah son of Iddo prophesied to the Jews in Judah and Jerusalem. They prophesied in the name of the God of Israel who was over them. Zerubbabel son of Shealtiel and Jeshua son of Jehozadak responded by starting again to rebuild the Temple of God in Jerusalem. And the prophets of God were with them and helped them" (Ezra 5:1-2).

DURING TIMES OF FRUSTRATION AND FEAR, ONLY the Word of God provides us with the power to overcome the obstacles that block our advancement. When work on the reconstruction of the Temple stopped, God sent two prophets to deliver His Word to the people to restore them and give them the strength and boldness they needed to continue the project. The book of Haggai says:

> *On August 29 of the second year of King Darius's reign, the Lord gave a message through the prophet Haggai to Zerubbabel son of Shealtiel, governor of Judah, and to Jeshua son of Jehozadak, the high priest.*
>
> *"This is what the Lord of Heaven's Armies says: 'The people are saying, "The time has not yet come to rebuild the house of the Lord."'*
>
> *Then the Lord sent this message through the prophet Haggai: "Why are you living in luxurious houses while my house lies in ruins?" This is what the Lord of Heaven's Armies says: "Look at what's happening to you! You have planted much but harvest little. You eat but are not satisfied. You drink but are still thirsty. You put on clothes but cannot keep warm. Your wages disappear as though you were putting them in pockets filled with holes!*
>
> *This is what the Lord of Heaven's Armies says: "Look at what's happening to you! Now go up into the hills, bring down timber, and rebuild my house. Then I will take pleasure in it and be honored, says the Lord. You hoped for rich*

harvests, but they were poor. And when you brought your harvest home, I blew it away. Why? Because my house lies in ruins, says the Lord of Heaven's Armies, while all of you are busy building your own fine houses. It's because of you that the heavens withhold the dew and the earth produces no crops. I have called for a drought on your fields and hills--a drought to wither the grain and grapes and olive trees and all your other crops, a drought to starve you and your livestock and to ruin everything you have worked so hard to get" (Haggai 1:1-11)

This was a strong Word from the Lord, but it was absolutely necessary for those who were comfortable with abandoning the work that the Lord had given them to do. These people needed to be shaken and stirred in spirit and awakened from their slumber. They were obeying man rather than God, and paying a heavy price for their disobedience.

Do you see any correlation between the way God's people were behaving in the days of Ezra, and the way they are behaving today? I certainly do, even though it pains me to admit it. All around us are people who say they are believers, and yet maintain that it is not the right time to act, return, repent or reconcile with God.

I believe this is why God has stirred my heart to write this book--so that as you read, your heart will be stirred as well and you will return to the Risen Savior. Am I equating myself with Ezra, or the prophet Haggai? Of course not. But I do know that God can and will use anyone who is open and willing to be used. And I also know that many of those who claim the title of "Christian" have become lethargic and apathetic about doing the work the Lord has called them to do.

So many people who go to church on Sunday morning don't give a thought to the Lord the rest of the week. He wants more from us than an hour or an hour and a half per week. There are 168 hours in a week, so if we tithed our time, that would mean that 16.8 hours would be spent in worship, study and service to the Lord each week.

I don't mean to imply that we should be legalistic with regard to the time we give to God. He wants our hearts, minds and souls--in other words, everything we are.

When the Father sent His prophet to speak to the children of Israel, He demanded to know why they were going all out on fixing their own homes when the house of the Lord was in ruins.

As the work resumed, the Lord watched over and blessed those who were facing opposition. He gave Zerubbabel and the other leaders the boldness and courage they needed to stand firm, no matter what opposition they faced. As you do His work you will be under His protection. I have no doubt about it! I have experienced His love, guidance and protection so many times during my ministry. I have learned that God will never give us a task to do without also giving us the strength, skill and wisdom to do it. His yoke is easy and His "demands" are never unreasonable.

The closer we are to God, the more aligned with His purposes, the less we will be distracted by opposition we face.

Love God more than His blessings

Many Christians pray that God will bless their finances and help them prosper, but when He does, they forget all about the God who answered their prayers, and fall in love with the blessings He provided. We have placed the God of the blessing behind the actual blessings instead of in front of them. This is why there are so many altars in ruins. People have given their hearts to earthly things instead of to the One who created those earthly things.

It is not a bad thing to prosper. On the contrary, prosperity is one of God's most beautiful blessings. But we must make sure that God's altar, meaning the human heart, is not far from Him.

The second portion of the word the prophet Haggai gave to the Children of Israel was to let them know that God was fully aware of what they were going through. He knew that they were eating but not feeling satisfied, getting paid but finding themselves without money, and waiting for a great harvest but ending up with the bare minimum. In other words, despite having everything in their favor to prosper, they endured a life of frustration and intimidation because they were not putting God first in their lives. They were not seeking His kingdom above everything else, but rather their own comfort and satisfaction. God had blocked their progress because they were not paying any attention to His agenda.

We must not let this happen to us. We must take an honest inventory of our lives and see where we are falling short in our service to the Lord. Are you making more money than ever before, but seeing that it won't go as far as it did when you were making less. That could be because of inflation. But more likely, it is because you are neglecting the altar of God that is within you.

Are you at a point in your life when you should be feeling safe and secure, but instead are always afraid? Do you feel as if your secure world is about to crumble all around you? That may be because you have lost your zeal for the things of God and left His altar in disrepair.

When you go to God in prayer, do you pray for the expansion and success of His Kingdom – or are your prayers for yourself and your family? I don't mean to imply that it's a bad thing to pray for your own needs, or the needs of your family and friends. We turn to God for these things because we understand that all blessings come from Him. There is nowhere else to turn and no one else to turn to. But if the Kingdom is uppermost in our minds, we will certainly pray that its borders will be enlarged and that thousands of lost souls will enter its gates each day.

Examine your life

The philosopher Socrates said that the unexamined life is not worth living. I'm not sure I would go that far. But I do think that every follower of Christ needs to stop frequently and take stock of whether his actions match up with his profession of faith in Christ. And when we do this, we have to be totally honest in our assessment, even if it hurts. I urge you to take a moment to reflect on these words from the Prophet Malachi:

> *Ever since the days of your ancestors, you have scorned my decrees and failed to obey them. Now return to me, and I will return to you, says the* LORD *of Heaven's Armies.*

> *But you ask, "How can we return when we have never gone away?"*

> *Should people cheat God? Yet you have cheated me! But you ask, "What do you mean? When did we ever cheat you?"*

You have cheated me of the tithes and offerings due to me. You are under a curse, for your whole nation has been cheating me. Bring all the tithes into the storehouse so there will be enough food in my Temple. If you do, says the Lord *of Heaven's Armies, I will open the windows of heaven for you. I will pour out a blessing so great you won't have enough room to take it in! Try it! Put me to the test! Your crops will be abundant, for I will guard them from insects and disease. Your grapes will not fall from the vine before they are ripe, says the* Lord *of Heaven's Armies. Then all nations will call you blessed, for your land will be such a delight, says the* Lord *of Heaven's Armies"* (Malachi 3:7-12).

We must do everything within our power to ensure that we are not cheating God. Please understand that I am not pointing at you or lecturing you. We are all in the same boat, so I am talking to myself as well as to dear friends like you. We all need to stop and take stock of our lives from time to time.

I think of the man the Bible calls "the rich young ruler." He came to Jesus and asked what he must do to obtain eternal life. When Jesus told him that he must obey the commandments, he responded that he had kept them since he was a youth. The rest of the story goes like this:

When Jesus heard his answer, he said, "There is still one thing you haven't done. Sell all your possessions and give the money to the poor, and you will have treasure in heaven. Then come, follow me."

But when the man heard this he became very sad, for he was very rich.

When Jesus saw this, he said, "How hard it is for the rich to enter the Kingdom of God! In fact, it is easier for a camel to go through the eye of a needle than for a rich person to enter the Kingdom of God!" (Luke 18:22-25)

Are we to infer from this passage that Jesus expects us to give away everything we own? No, not unless our material wealth is more important to us than God. God deserves and expects to be number one in our lives. If there is anything in our lives that takes precedence over our *relationship with God, we need to get rid of it.*

There could be areas in our lives that we haven't surrendered to God. There may be things we need to work on, deliver, change, and fix, and until we do, we will not experience the peace God gives--the peace that passes all understanding.

Responding to the challenge

When God saw that His people had heard His words and had reacted by re-starting the work on the Temple, He again spoke to them through Haggai: "Then Haggai, the LORD's messenger, gave the people this message from the LORD: "I am with you, says the LORD!" (Haggai 1:13). This is why in Ezra 5:5, it says: "But because their God was watching over them, the leaders of the Jews were not prevented from building until a report was sent to Darius and he returned his decision."

When you walk in obedience, you activate God's coverage. There is blessing in obedience. It was time to rebuild God's Temple. It wasn't too early or too late. This was the time God desired. Untimely obedience is also disobedience. This is why it's important to remember that when God has a purpose with someone, nothing will interfere with what He has planned.

Afterward, the very same people who tried to stop the works of the Temple witnessed another beautiful reality. When Tattenai saw they were rebuilding the Temple, he went to accuse them of going against the order to stop the works, but they recited the decree that King Cyrus had established. They also spoke with clarity about the history of the Temple. They told of the people's disobedience, how God had allowed King Nebuchadnezzar to destroy the Temple, and how God now, through King Cyrus, had given them the opportunity to abandon the captivity to rebuild their shattered city. They spoke about God's truth that is far beyond men's reality.　`

Greater things are yet to come

When the children of Israel rebuilt the ruins, God spoke to them again through the prophet Haggai, saying:

> "Say this to Zerubbabel son of Shealtiel, governor of Judah, and to Jeshua, son of Jehozadak, the high priest, and to the remnant of God's people there in the land: 'Does anyone remember this house--this Temple--in its former splendor? How, in comparison, does it look to you now? It must seem like nothing at all! But now the LORD says: Be strong, Zerubbabel. Be strong, Jeshua son of Jehozadak, the high priest. Be strong, all you people still left in the land. And now get to work, for I am with you, says the LORD of Heaven's Armies. My Spirit remains among you, just as I promised when you came out of Egypt. So do not be afraid.'

> "For this is what the LORD of Heaven's Armies says: In just a little while I will again shake the heavens and the earth, the oceans and the dry land. I will shake all the nations, and the treasures of all the nations

will be brought to this Temple. I will fill this place with glory, says the LORD of Heaven's Armies. The silver is mine, and the gold is mine, says the LORD of Heaven's Armies. The future glory of this Temple will be greater than its past glory, says the LORD of Heaven's Armies. And in this place I will bring peace. I, the LORD of Heaven's Armies, have spoken!" (Haggai 2:2–9).

What a beautiful promise. In the King James Version, this passage reads as follows:

"The glory of this latter house shall be greater than of the former," saith the Lord of hosts: "and in this place will I give peace, saith the Lord of hosts."

You see, when we give our all to God, He takes it and makes it more beautiful than we ever could have imagined. Jehovah was telling His people that no matter how good or pleasant the past had been, the future was sure to be even better. When the work was done, when they walked in obedience and fulfilled the assignment God had given them, then the glory of the latter days would be manifested.

This was how it was 3,000 years ago, and this is how it is today. If we turn our hearts to God and reconstruct the ruins while living under obedience, a greater glory will surely come to us.

This is the emphasis of the prophet Zechariah, who was sent by God at this time to tell God's people, "Return to me, and I will return to you." (Zechariah 1:3) This is, in essence, the same message that was given several hundred years later by the Lord's brother James, who wrote:

> *Come close to God, and God will come close to you. Wash your hands, you sinners; purify your hearts, for your loyalty is divided between God and the world. Let there be tears for what you have done. Let there be sorrow and deep grief. Let there be sadness instead of laughter, and gloom instead of joy. Humble yourselves before the Lord, and he will lift you up in honor. (James 4:8-10.)*

God sent another the prophet Zechariah, and he spoke to the people with power and authority: "Therefore, say to the people, 'This is what the Lord of Heaven's Armies says: Return to me, and I will return to you, says the Lord of Heaven's Armies'" (Zechariah 1:3).

God is expressing His desire to see His lost sheep return to the fold. Just before Jesus went to His excruciatingly painful death on the cross, He looked out over the city of Jerusalem and said, *"O Jerusalem, Jerusalem, the city that kills the prophets and stones God's messengers! How often I have wanted to gather your children together as a hen protects her chicks beneath her wings, but you wouldn't let me"* (Matthew 23:37). His heart was broken, not for Himself, but for the unrepentant people of Jerusalem. This is the same heart He has for His people today. He weeps for us when we turn away from the salvation only He can offer, and is always ready to welcome His children home.

No one is excluded from God's grace and mercy. The apostle Paul referred to himself as "the chief of sinners," and that seems to be a fair description. Before he became a follower of Christ, he devoted himself to persecuting God's people. As Christians were being tortured and killed for their faith in those days, it seems likely that Paul was guilty of murder, or at the very least of being an accessory to murder. And yet He went on to write nearly one-fourth of the entire New Testament.

Do you know someone who says, "You don't know the things I've done. God could never forgive and accept me."

If so, I urge you to let them know that this is pure nonsense. Have they done things worse than Paul did before he encountered Jesus on the road to Damascus? Surely not. And yet, Paul became one of the great builders of the kingdom of God.

There are so many other examples. I think of a man named Tom Tarrants. Tarrants was once a top soldier in the Ku Klux Klan. He was responsible for bombings of

Jewish organizations, synagogues and black churches across the southern United States. He was seriously wounded in a gun battle with the FBI and then sentenced to life in prison without the possibility of parole. Tarrants hated Jews and blacks, and if I had met him, he almost certainly would have hated me because of my Hispanic heritage. He hated anyone who wasn't white.

But in prison, Tarrants began reading the Bible. He was touched by the unconditional love of Christ. He came to understand Paul's words in Galatians 3:28, *"There is no longer Jew or Gentile, slave or free, male and female. For you are all one in Christ Jesus."*

Tom Tarrants was completely changed by the love of Jesus and the power of the Holy Spirit. And, through a series of what can only be described as miracles, he was released from prison. He went on to pastor a large inter-racial church in Washington, D.C. He has devoted his life to serving Jesus and working for racial reconciliation.

In Ezra's day, he would have been working on the front lines of the rebuilding of the Temple, shoulder to shoulder with the Levites who had served God all their lives.

Zechariah's Amazing Vision

Before we move on to talk about the benefits of obedience, I want to take just a few minutes to talk about an important vision God gave to Zechariah. The prophet writes:

> *Then the angel who had been talking with me returned and woke me, as though I had been asleep. "What do you see now?" he asked.*
>
> *I answered, "I see a solid gold lampstand with a bowl of oil on top of it. Around the bowl are seven lamps, each having seven spouts with wicks. And I see two olive trees, one on each side of the bowl." Then I asked the angel, "What are these, my lord? What do they mean?"*
>
> *"Don't you know?" the angel asked.*
>
> *"No, my lord," I replied.*
>
> *Then he said to me, "This is what the LORD says to Zerubbabel: It is not by force nor by strength, but by my Spirit, says the LORD of Heaven's Armies. Nothing, not even a mighty mountain, will stand in Zerubbabel's way; it will become a level plain before him! And when Zerubbabel sets the final stone of the Temple in place, the people will shout: 'May God bless it! May God bless it!'"* (Zechariah 4:1–7)

This was a clear message to those on the frontlines of the work in Jerusalem. Once again, God had to awaken the hearts that were in slumber.

The angel was also trying to make Zechariah understand that the reconstruction of the Temple would require more than just natural strengths and capacities. This assignment would require people who could rely exclusively on the power of the Holy Ghost--men and women who were willing to be a channel of anointing that only comes from the Holy One of Israel.

In his vision, Zechariah saw something he had never seen before in the Temple: two olive trees that provided seven lamps with oil through seven tubes. One of the most tedious jobs in the Temple was the tending of the lamps of the gold candelabras. They had to be continuously refilled with oil and cleansed. In his vision, Zechariah saw an "auto-refill" in which the lamps were being filled by the olive trees. In the Temple, the lamps were relit with pure olive oil specially prepared to be used in the Temple. This is why Zechariah asked for an explanation of the vision.

Zechariah saw the vision but didn't understand what it meant. What he saw was simple but very unusual: a candelabra filled directly with olive oil by the two trees.

In the Bible, the Holy Spirit is also represented by oil. In other words, the oil that we need to fulfill God's work does not come through our own strength or capacity but from God. It would not be through man's intelligence, capability, or physical force that the Temple would be rebuilt, but rather, through the Spirit of the Lord.

In December of 2019 this was precisely the word that the Holy Spirit whispered in my heart as I waited before Him in prayer: "Not by might, nor by power, but by my Spirit, says the Lord of hosts." It is the reason why I wrote this book to remind the family of God that when works are completed by human effort, we take all of the credit, but when they are accomplished through a continuous flow of the Spirit, then it all is for the grace and glory of God. It is precisely through God's grace that we are able to face life's obstacles with the conviction that we will overcome.

Lesson #7 from the Book of Ezra

When Ezra returned to Jerusalem, he was astonished by the spiritual poverty he found there. Most of the people had completely lost touch with God. They didn't know His commands. They had never read the Scriptures, and probably didn't even know they existed. That makes me wonder: Is America losing touch with God's Word. Did you know that only 11 percent of Americans read the Bible each day? Or that 29 percent say they never read the Bible at all? These are discouraging numbers for sure. But the Barna Research Group, which compiled these numbers in 2021, reports that these number are actually better than in previous years and the Bible is gaining in popularity. Let's do what we can to help these positive trends continue. Read your Bible daily. Urge others to do the same. And never be ashamed of God's Word. Always remember that His Word "is a lamp unto our feet and a light unto our path" (Psalm 119:105 KJV).

QUESTIONS FOR SPIRITUAL REFLECTION

1. Do you make it a habit to remember the prophetic words spoken over you? How does remembering those words impact you.

2. When have you felt God's protection in your life?

3. Have you ever seen anything come to a stop because of an act of disobedience?

4. When you compare yourself with the person you were five, ten or fifteen years ago, how can you see that you have changed?

____

____

____

5. Mention at least three victories you have achieved with God's help.

____

____

____

8

THE REWARDS OF OBEDIENCE

So the Jewish elders continued their work, and they were greatly encouraged by the preaching of the prophets Haggai and Zechariah son of Iddo. The Temple was finally finished, as had been commanded by the God of Israel and decreed by Cyrus, Darius, and Artaxerxes, the kings of Persia. (Ezra 6:14).

THE BIBLE HAS A GREAT DEAL TO SAY ABOUT THE blessings that come to those who live in obedience to God. In the 28th chapter of Deuteronomy, we find some powerful words on this subject. These are words that Moses spoke to the Children of Israel after learning from God that he was about to die. The great prophet knew that every word he spoke at this time was vitally important. His goal was to give God's people a message that would stay with them and guide them as they moved into the Promised Land, and far beyond. He gave this word on the importance of obedience:

> *"You will experience all these blessings if you*
> *obey the LORD your God:*
>
> *"Your towns and your fields will be blessed.*
> *Your children and your crops*
> *will be blessed.*
> *The offspring of your herds and flocks*
> *will be blessed.*
> *Your fruit baskets and breadboards*
> *will be blessed.*
> *Wherever you go and whatever you do,*
> *you will be blessed.*
>
> *"The LORD will conquer your enemies when they*
> *attack you. They will attack you from one direc-*
> *tion, but they will scatter from you in seven!*
>
> *"The LORD will guarantee a blessing on every-*
> *thing you do and will fill your storehouses with*
> *grain. The LORD your God will bless you in the*
> *land he is giving you."*

The list of blessings for obedience goes on and on. I urge you to read it for yourself and be encouraged. But then Moses had some scary words for those who refuse to obey God's commands:

> *"But if you refuse to listen to the* LORD *your God*
> *and do not obey all the commands and decrees I*
> *am giving you today, all these curses will come*
> *and overwhelm you:*

> *'Your towns and your fields*
> *will be cursed.*
> *Your fruit baskets and breadboards*
> *will be cursed.*
> *Your children and your crops*
> *will be cursed.*
> *The offspring of your herds and flocks*
> *will be cursed.*
> *Wherever you go and whatever you do,*
> *you will be cursed.*

> *"The* LORD *himself will send on you curses, con-*
> *fusion, and frustration in everything you do,*
> *until at last you are completely destroyed for*
> *doing evil and abandoning me."*

As I said in the last chapter, obedience brings forth blessings. This is exactly what started to occur when the children of Israel were working full blast on the works of God. Ezra and the others who had returned to Judah were doing everything they could to obey what God had instructed them to do, but a new king had come to the throne in Babylon and he had ordered that the work be stopped.

What were they to do?

Wait for God to fight for them, which is exactly what He did!

In 522 B.C. the reign of Artaxerxes (otherwise known as Cambyses) came to an end, after only seven years, and a swift victory over Egypt that elevated him to hero status. Scholars aren't sure how the king died. Some believe he took his own life, but others say that he most likely died in an accident. Whichever it was, we can be sure that God removed him from power to pave the way for the Temple's reconstruction. Upon his death, he was replaced by Darius, who was noted for his administrative genius, his great building projects and his benevolence toward the nations that had been conquered and absorbed into the Persian Empire.

Shortly after He ascended to the throne, Darius called for the archives that were being stored and conserved in the treasury at Babylon. He was astounded to read the following words:

> *"Let the Temple be rebuilt on the site where Jews used to offer their sacrifices, using the original foundations. Its height will be ninety feet, and its width will be ninety feet. Every three layers*

of specially prepared stones will be topped by a layer of timber. All expenses will be paid by the royal treasury. Furthermore, the gold and silver cups, which were taken to Babylon by Nebuchadnezzar from the Temple of God in Jerusalem, must be returned to Jerusalem and put back where they belong. Let them be taken back to the Temple of God." (Ezra 6:3–5).

The new king was shocked when he discovered that this work had not been carried out, but rather abandoned due to the order from his predecessor. When the king saw the gravity of the situation, he wrote to the same people who had provoked the initial opposition against the Israelites and told them:

Now therefore, Tattenai, governor of the province west of the Euphrates River, and Shethar-bozenai, and your colleagues and other officials west of the Euphrates River--stay away from there! Do not disturb the construction of the Temple of God. Let it be rebuilt on its original site, and do not hinder the governor of Judah and the elders of the Jews in their work.

Moreover, I hereby decree that you are to help these elders of the Jews as they rebuild this Temple of God. You must pay the full construction costs, without delay, from my taxes collected in the province west of the Euphrates River so that the work will not be interrupted.

Give the priests in Jerusalem whatever is needed in the way of young bulls, rams, and male lambs for the burnt offerings presented to the God of heaven. And without fail, provide them with as much wheat, salt, wine, and olive oil as they need each day. Then they will be able to offer acceptable sacrifices to the God of heaven and pray for the welfare of the king and his sons.

Those who violate this decree in any way will have a beam pulled from their house. Then they will be lifted up and impaled on it, and their house will be reduced to a pile of rubble. May the God who has chosen the city of Jerusalem as the place to honor his name destroy any king or nation that violates this command and destroys this Temple.

I, Darius, have issued this decree. Let it be obeyed with all diligence. (Ezra 6:6-12)

Once again, God had turned a curse into a blessing. The same people who opposed the children of Israel became the witnesses of the new decree King Darius was about to establish in their favor.

This testifies to what is written in Psalm 23, where the Scriptures talk of God serving a banquet to his children in the presence of their enemies. Not only were Tattenai and Bozenai called to be witnesses of the new decree, but they also received strict instructions to "stay away from there," and stop causing trouble for the Jews. This is just one of the many benefits we receive when we decide to turn back to God: Justice and mercy poured upon us in front of our enemies.

When we walk under God's justice, He makes sure that everything falls into place. He will use whomever He chooses to make sure we are blessed. It's not always easy to see how God is working behind the scenes, but if we remain in Him, we will see the pieces fall into place, and He will show us His divine justice. Even if we don't always have an answer to the "why," if we trust the Lord's plans for our lives, believing they are good and not evil, we will see the fulfillment of His promises to us.

I believe that most of us will never know, until we get to heaven, all the ways God has blessed and protected us in this life. And when we do finally see all the ways He has watched over and blessed us, I know we're going to be amazed. You may be shocked to see all the times he protected you from getting into an automobile accident. You may have been starting a trip, walked out to your car, and then remembered you'd left something in the house and had to go back in and get it. Perhaps you were annoyed over that delay--but the few minutes it took to go back in the house could have protected you from being hit by a drunk driver or suffering some other calamity. How many times has God protected you from other kinds of trouble-- being injured in some way other than a car crash, being scammed, getting robbed, and so forth? I think we need to thank God for all the ways He has blessed us that we didn't see.

For example, a pastor was on a long trip by car. He felt weary so he turned off into a rest area to rest for a few minutes. Afterwards, as he was getting ready to pull back onto the Expressway, he looked both ways and saw that the road looked clear. But suddenly, for some reason, he felt that he needed to stop. He slammed on the breaks and just managed to avoid being flattened by a semi that rocketed past. How had he missed seeing that truck? He sat there for a few minutes, trembling over the close call he had experienced. He knew that it was only by the grace of God that He was well and alive.

A young lady remembers the morning when she was late to school. She grabbed her books, ran out the door and prepared to run across the street, without looking. As she stepped off the curb and into the street, she felt a pair of unseen hands pushing her back. She toppled backwards onto the sidewalk, shaken but unhurt as a car zoomed past. If not for those unseen hands, she would have been hit and seriously injured or killed. Our God protects and blesses us in so many ways!

Perhaps you've heard about what happened at the West Side Baptist Church in Beatrice, Nebraska, way back on Wednesday, March 1, 1950.[11] Choir practice was due to begin at 7:20 that evening. But for various reasons, all 15 members of the choir were late. For that reason, no one was injured or killed when a gas explosion destroyed the church at 7:25. The blast was so strong that it shattered windows in neighboring homes and knocked a radio station off the air.

None of the reason for the choir members' lateness were serious. Two women couldn't get their car to start. The pastor and his wife and daughter were late because they discovered at the last minute that a dress needed ironing. Another was detained by a phone call that came just as she was walking out the door. And one choir member decided to take a short nap and overslept. And so it went.

According to the Snopes website, which verified the event, past performance indicated that each person would be late for choir practice one in four times. Thus, the odds that they would all be late on the same night were one million to one.[12]

---

[11] Medium.com / the mystery box, "How 15 mundane miracles saved 15 lives from an explosion," by Martina Petkova, September 11, 2020

[12] Snopes.com, "Church Explosion Spares Choir," December 31, 1998

The moral of the story: Don't ever be upset by those small annoyances that sometime make us late. They may just be God's way of saving your life.

God provides all our needs

In addition to providing physical coverage and protection, God ensured the financial support of the reconstruction of the Temple. In King Darius's decree, he establishes that all costs related to the reconstruction of the Temple must be covered by the king's treasury. That money would come from the same provinces these enemies of the Jews came from.

How like our Heavenly Father. The Word of God is full of such provision promises for His children. Philippians 4:19, says: "And this same God who takes care of me will supply all your needs from his glorious riches, which have been given to us in Christ Jesus." And 2 Corinthians 9:8, says: "And God will generously provide all you need. Then you will always have everything you need and plenty left over to share with others."

Another promise is found in Proverbs 13:22: "Good people leave an inheritance to their grandchildren, but the sinner's wealth passes to the godly." If you keep looking, you will continue to find more promises. We serve a generous God.

One of the beautiful things about being a child of God is knowing that our Heavenly Father is aware of our needs. As David wrote in Psalm 37:25, "I have never seen the godly abandoned or their children begging for bread." God prepared for every detail beforehand as part of His reconciliation with His people. That is the God I am presenting to you in these lines, a God who loves you and will not give up in calling you to His presence.

It is only when we finally enter His presence and reestablish our relationship with Him that we will see the victory.

> *So the Jewish elders continued their work, and they were greatly encouraged by the preaching of the prophets Haggai and Zechariah son of Iddo. The Temple was finally finished, as had been commanded by the God of Israel and decreed by Cyrus, Darius, and Artaxerxes, the kings of Persia. The Temple was completed on March 12, during the sixth year of King Darius's reign. (Ezra 6:14-15)*

Everything would turn out all right for the Children of Israel because they were walking in obedience.

I have said it many times before and I will say it again: There is blessing and prosperity in obedience. When we refer to prosperity, most people automatically assume we are speaking about material things or money. Real prosperity is not about earthly things, but spiritual richness. For this reason, God spoke to Joshua, saying: *"Study this Book of Instruction continually meditate on it day and night so you will be sure to obey everything written in it. Only then will you prosper and succeed in all you do."* (Joshua 1:8). One thing is for sure, God desires to prosper His people as He prospers their souls.

Needed: People for the Temple

Once the place of worship was restored, the order and positions for the services were established as required by the law of Moses. It would make no sense to have a Temple established without people there to serve those who would come seeking restoration in the house of the Lord. It was important to establish this order in the Temple so that God's purposes were fulfilled. The servers and priests chosen for the Temple's services went through a purification process, as God commanded them to do.

There are many reasons why people come to the altar. Some come for salvation. Others come to rededicate their lives to the Lord. And still others come to surrender their past, get rid of old habits and old ways of thinking and living. We impart what we carry, so it is important that we live each day in sanctity so we can fulfill our priestly duties within our community of faith.

1 Peter 2:9 tells us, *"You are royal priests, a holy nation, God's very own possession. As a result, you can show others*

the goodness of God, for he called you out of the darkness into his wonderful light." We must purify ourselves by going to the altar and then being ready to minister to others who come in need of God's grace and mercy.

Salvation is received immediately when we accept Jesus as Savior. But sanctification is an everyday process, and it evolves as we surrender ourselves to the Lord and grant the Holy Ghost permission to do in us His great works. It is a calling to come to the altar and surrender all of what we are: body, soul, and spirit to the Father.

We must not take lightly the sanctity that the Temple requires. Paul described it in his letter to *Timothy:*

> *If someone aspires to be a church leader, he desires an honorable position. So a church leader must be a man whose life is above reproach. He must be faithful to his wife. He must exercise self-control, live wisely, and have a good reputation. He must enjoy having guests in his home, and he must be able to teach. He must not be a heavy drinker or be violent. He must be gentle, not quarrelsome, and not love money. He must manage his own family well, having children who respect and obey him. For if a man cannot manage his own household, how can he take care of God's church?*

A church leader must not be a new believer, because he might become proud, and the devil would cause him to fall. Also, people outside the church must speak well of him so that he will not be disgraced and fall into the devil's trap.

In the same way, deacons must be well respected and have integrity. They must not be heavy drinkers or dishonest with money. They must be committed to the mystery of the faith now revealed and must live with a clear conscience. Before they are appointed as deacons, let them be closely examined. If they pass the test, then let them serve as deacons.

In the same way, their wives must be respected and must not slander others. They must exercise self-control and be faithful in everything they do.

A deacon must be faithful to his wife, and he must manage his children and household well. Those who do well as deacons will be rewarded with respect from others and will have increased confidence in their faith in Christ Jesus (1 Timothy 3:1–13).

God is clear about how He wants us to live. His Word explains His expectations for us and tells us what we can do to shine as His representatives and ambassadors here on earth.

Lesson #8 from the Book of Ezra

We can learn so much from looking at the life of a godly man like Ezra. One of the things we can learn is the value of obedience. When God called Ezra to go to Jerusalem, he obeyed without question. King David wrote, "I have hidden your word in my heart, so that I might not sin against you" (Psalm 119:11). Ezra too, had hidden God's Word in His heart. He had memorized the entire law, and could quote it or write it any time he was asked. Anyone who wants to walk in obedience needs to have a thorough understanding of the Scriptures. I'm not saying you should memorize the entire Bible. I doubt if anyone could do that. But it is important to know what God says about salvation, our relationship with Him and other people, how He expects us to live, etc. If you haven't been reading the Bible regularly, and meditating on the truths it contains, I urge you start right now. It will help you walk in obedience, and change your entire life for the better.

QUESTIONS FOR SPIRITUAL REFLECTION

1. How have you felt when successfully completing one of the assignments God has given you?

2. How have you seen God's provision in your life?

3. Are you able to identify at least three friends or family members whose hearts you can help restore and bring them closer to Jesus?

4. What old ways of thinking – if any – do you need to
    eradicate from your life?

____

____

____

5. What steps will you to take to cleanse yourself of
    wrong ways of thinking.

____

____

____

9

BE READY TO TEACH

Ezra arrived in Jerusalem in August of that year. He had arranged to leave Babylon on April 8, the first day of the new year, and he arrived at Jerusalem on August 4, for the gracious hand of his God was on him. This was because Ezra had determined to study and obey the Law of the LORD and to teach those decrees and regulations to the people of Israel. (Ezra 7:8-10).

ARE YOU CONCERNED ABOUT IMPACTING OTHERS for the Lord? Ezra certainly was. And if you don't really care about the millions of lost souls out there, I urge you to ask the Lord to give you compassion for them. I once heard a preacher say that no one goes to Heaven alone. In other words, in order to get there, you must be taking someone with you.

I think that's a good point, even though I'm not sure I agree. The only thing you have to do to get to Heaven is accept Jesus Christ as your Lord and Savior. On the other hand, if Jesus has changed your life, then you certainly want to tell others about that and give them a chance to experience the joy and hope He gives.

What would you do if you woke up one morning and saw that smoke was pouring out of your neighbor's house? Would you draw your blinds and go on about your business, ignoring the fact that your neighbors might burn to death unless you warned them?

I don't think so. I think you'd call 911 to report the fire, and then run to your neighbor's house, shouting, "Your house is on fire! Get out! Fire!" You'd keep shouting and pounding on their front door until they were safely out of danger.

What is my point? That people all around us are lost and in danger of spending eternity in hell, and they need us to warn them, to prevent them from winding up eternally separated from God.

In other words, we need to have the passion and zeal of Ezra and always be ready to share God's Word.

When Paul wrote to his young protégé Timothy, he said, *"You have heard me teach things that have been confirmed by many reliable witnesses. Now teach these truths to other trustworthy people who will be able to pass them on to others."* (2 Timothy 2:2) We don't have to stop there.

We could continue, ". . .teach these truths to other trustworthy people who will be able to pass them on to others. . .who will be able to pass them onto others. . .who will be able to pass them on to others. . ." and so on, until the entire world has had an opportunity to hear the gospel.

Ezra renovates a nation

Ezra served as God's instrument to spiritually renovate a nation. His life serves as an example for all who have been called to be instruments of change. He gives us the formula needed today in each church, pulpit, and by every leader. Real restoration will begin in us when we seek to help others renovate and restore themselves.

Do you see the secret behind Ezra's success? The Bible says that he was determined to study and obey the decrees of the Lord before he began teaching those decrees and regulations to others. Like Ezra, we have to apply what we learn from God and His Word before we start trying to help others. In other words, we need to be sure that we have been changed before we can go out and change others. Sometimes we make the mistake of wanting to help others before we have applied these lessons to ourselves. The formula for success in ministry is clear: learn first and apply it to our lives so that we can later teach others.

We all carry a calling from God since we have all been recruited as part of the Great Commission:

> *Therefore, go and make disciples of all the nations, baptizing them in the name of the Father and the Son and the Holy Spirit. Teach these new disciples to obey all the commands I have given you. And be sure of this: I am with you always, even to the end of the age. (Matthew 28:19–20).*

Chapter seven of the book of Ezra opens the way to one of the most rewarding ministries of the church, the ministry of Teaching. This chapter goes into more detail describing this great man of God, describing all of his ancestors all the way back to Aaron, the brother of Moses and the first high priest. The Scriptures tell us the following about Ezra. "This Ezra was a scribe who was well versed in the Law of Moses, which the LORD, the God of Israel, had given to the people of Israel. He came up to Jerusalem from Babylon, and the king gave him everything he asked for, because the gracious hand of the LORD his God was on him" (Ezra 7:6).

Ezra was a doctor and interpreter of Hebrew law. We can say that Ezra was a man of God who made sure the mandates of the Lord were fulfilled. God was with him.

When he left for Jerusalem in obedience to God's calling on his life, he didn't go alone.

> *"Some of the people of Israel, as well as some of the priests, Levites, singers, gatekeepers, and Temple servants, traveled up to Jerusalem with him in the seventh year of King Artaxerxes' reign." (Ezra 7:7)*

Ezra knew exactly what his mission was. He understood that he was responsible for establishing the order God was demanding of his people. The Word doesn't explain why Ezra wasn't among the first group of people who traveled to Jerusalem from Babylonia. Nevertheless, Ezra was right in the center of God's will. God knew his name and was using him to fulfill His purposes.

I want to assure you that God knows your name, too. He is well aware of your strengths and abilities and sees your efforts on behalf of His kingdom.

The devil wants us to feel like no one has noticed what we have to offer. He loves it when we are down because discouragement leads to powerlessness.

Always remember that God has blessed you with gifts, talents, and fruits that are needed for the service of His people. Just as God called Ezra into His service, He is pronouncing your name, and will use kings, governors, people in authority, and everyday people to let you know

He is calling you. When we respond to the call of God, we are going to thrive and prosper. When we reject his calling, we will wither and die. As Jesus said, *"Even now the ax of God's judgment is poised, ready to sever the roots of the trees. Yes, every tree that does not produce good fruit will be chopped down and thrown into the fire."* (Matthew 3:10)

How many people who were once skilled Bible teachers are now estranged from the house of the Lord? How many men and women who once mentored younger believers have forsaken the purpose for which God commissioned them? How many who once boldly proclaimed the Gospel now sit in silence?

In Jerusalem during the days of Ezra there were many thousands of Jews who had lost their way. They had intermingled with the heathen tribes that surrounded them. They had also mingled the truths of the scriptures with the myths, legends and abominable practices of the neighboring peoples. They desperately needed someone like Ezra to bring them back to God.

We're just talking about the fact that God knew Ezra by name. So, apparently, did the King of Persia, Artaxerxes. He was aware of Ezra's character and trusted his judgment. This was evident in the letter the king sent to Ezra:

> *From Artaxerxes, the king of kings, to Ezra the priest, the teacher of the law of the God of heaven. Greetings.*

I decree that any of the people of Israel in my kingdom, including the priests and Levites, may volunteer to return to Jerusalem with you. I and my council of seven hereby instruct you to conduct an inquiry into the situation in Judah and Jerusalem, based on your God's law, which is in your hand. We also commission you to take with you silver and gold, which we are freely presenting as an offering to the God of Israel who lives in Jerusalem.

Furthermore, you are to take any silver and gold that you may obtain from the province of Babylon, as well as the voluntary offerings for the people and the priests that are presented for the Temple of their God in Jerusalem. These donations are to be used specifically for the purchase of bulls, rams, male lambs, and the appropriate grain offerings and liquid offerings, all of which will be offered on the altar of the Temple of your God in Jerusalem. Any silver and gold that is left over may be used in whatever way you and your colleagues feel is the will of your God.

Furthermore, you are to take any silver and gold that you may obtain from the province of Babylon, as well as the voluntary offerings for the people and the priests that are presented for the Temple of their God in Jerusalem. These donations are to be used specifically for the purchase of bulls, rams, male lambs, and the appropriate grain offerings and liquid offerings, all of which will be offered on the altar of the Temple of your God in Jerusalem. Any silver and gold that is left over may be used in whatever way you and your colleagues feel is the will of your God.

But as for the cups we are entrusting to you for the service of the Temple of your God, deliver them all to the God of Jerusalem. If you need anything else for your God's Temple or for any similar needs, you may take it from the royal treasury.

I, Artaxerxes the king, hereby send this decree to all the treasurers in the province west of the Euphrates River: 'You are to give Ezra, the priest and teacher of the law of the God of heaven, whatever he requests of you. . . Be careful to provide whatever the God of heaven demands for his Temple, for why should we risk bringing God's anger against the realm of the king and his sons? I also decree that no priest, Levite, singer, gatekeeper, Temple servant, or other worker in this Temple of God will be required to pay tribute, customs, or tolls of any kind.'

> *And you, Ezra, are to use the wisdom your*
> *God has given you to appoint magistrates and*
> *judges who know your God's laws to govern all*
> *the people in the province west of the Euphrates*
> *River. Teach the law to anyone who does not*
> *know it. Anyone who refuses to obey the law*
> *of your God and the law of the king will be*
> *punished immediately, either by death, banish-*
> *ment, confiscation of goods, or imprisonment.*
> *(Ezra 7:12-26)*

Wow! What an amazing and revealing letter. The king's words should be enough to stir the hearts of all who hear them, and wake those who have fallen into spiritual slumber. The Bible doesn't go into details about what Ezra was doing when he received the king's letter--but it's amazing to see how God revealed to the king that it was the correct time for Ezra to return to his rightful place. God already had this season planned for Ezra. He knew the precise moment he would move Ezra to Jerusalem to fulfill his purpose.

God will never forsake you

Another thing we learn from the story of Ezra is that when God calls a person, He enables and supports him. As He says in His word, God will never forsake or abandon us. He will never give you a calling He is not willing to fulfill, either by using you as His representative or by enabling you. If God has called you as a missionary, He will take care of all your needs and guard your family while you walk in obedience. He will empower you and bless your efforts.

This same letter we've been talking about in this chapter is a dedication from God to you. It is the Holy Spirit placing a calling on your heart so that you can return to Him.

For the second time in history, we see that when God stirred the heart of a king, he established a decree open to anyone who desired to leave Babylonia and the state of captivity. Therefore, when Ezra left for Jerusalem, he took with him priests, teachers, and servers who had not responded to the initial calling issued by Darius. God lifted a leader who simultaneously responded to the calling and motivated other leaders to return to the altar as well.

Will you be like Ezra? Will you inspire others to respond to God's calling. Christianity is not a spectator sport, but too many of God's children are watching from the bleachers when God wants them to be out on the field, playing in the game. God doesn't need any more fans; He needs more players. Matthew 9:37–38 says, "He said to his disciples, 'The harvest is great, but the workers are few. So pray to the Lord who is in charge of the harvest; ask him to send more workers into his fields.'"

There is an urgent need for workers, ministers, and those called to preach the Word of God, to restore and love those God loves. No parent is at peace when they see their children drifting away from God; how much more does our Heavenly Father suffer watching His children wander far from His presence? It's time to return to the altar, respond to the calling, and help others do the same.

We are called to be watchmen

In his letter, King Artaxerxes gave Ezra the responsibility of verifying that the children of God called to restore the ruins were actually fulfilling God's will. This is yet another controversial situation in which we find ourselves today. Many want to profess as prophets but only with a soft word, promises, and good news on behalf of God. When they have to establish order, discipline, and expose sins, they prefer to remain silent. We now see motivational sermons from the pulpit instead of messages that confront our lifestyles and spiritual conditions. When God says to prophesy of blessings to come and rivers of living water, we certainly have to report what He says. But we cannot ignore it when God speaks of the necessity for repentance, or impending judgment. We cannot tell people, "God says everything is just wonderful," when He hasn't said that at all.

We are called to be watchmen over those who have come to the altar. Those of us who are strong in the faith must shepherd them and ensure that they are walking in paths of righteousness. I don't mean that we should spy on our brothers and sisters and keep tabs on every wrong thing they do. There's a difference between being a spiritual policeman and a watchman. A policeman arrests people and puts them in jail. A watchman warns people when they are in danger. He or she leads people back to holy living in the most loving and kind way possible.

A watchman is like the Good Shepherd who, when he or she sees a lamb that has strayed away and is in danger, goes after it and brings it back to the fold. He or she is like the Good Shepherd, who leaves the 99 sheep who are safely in the fold and goes out in search of the one lamb who is lost.

It's not easy to leave the safety of the fold, or the fellowship of the 99 sheep who love the Lord and are growing stronger in their faith every day. But God calls us to go, and so go we must!

Before we move on, I want to talk just a little bit more about the Gift of Prophecy. This has always been one of the most important Gifts of the Spirit, but it has also been a bit problematic. Why? For one thing, it is easy to get excited and carried away, and prophesy things that we want to see happen, even though God has not said a thing about them.

I think this was happening even in the first century, and that's why Paul wrote, "Do not scoff at prophecies, but test everything that is said" (I Thessalonians 20:21).

And John wrote in 1 John 4:1, "Dear friends, do not believe everyone who claims to speak by the Spirit. You must test them to see if the spirit they have comes from God. For there are many false prophets in the world."

Even so, Paul wrote, "Let love be your highest goal! But you should also desire the special abilities the Spirit gives--especially the ability to prophesy" (1Corinthians 14:1)

So, to sum it all up, we are to desire the

Gift of Prophecy, but must be very sure

God is speaking through us before we claim something as a prophecy.

Ezra on a mission

Ezra was on a mission to restore the order God demanded in His house. Even though our God moves within disorder, He does it to establish order. God has always been a demanding, jealous God full of details. When He gives instructions, He gives them full of details. So, Ezra's assignment was hard. Within the king's letter to Ezra there is a very important disclaimer regarding the assignment Ezra had received. Ezra 7:19 says:

> *Furthermore, you are to take any silver and gold that you may obtain from the province of Babylon, as well as the voluntary offerings for the people and the priests that are presented for the Temple of their God in Jerusalem. These donations are to be used specifically for the purchase of bulls, rams, male lambs, and the appropriate grain offerings and liquid offerings, all of which will be offered on the altar of the Temple of your God in Jerusalem. Any silver and gold that is left over may be used in whatever way you and your colleagues feel is the will of your God.*

Ezra was responsible for collecting all donations and offerings destined to cover the needs of the reconstruction of the Temple.

We are all called to place sacrifices upon the altar through worship, offerings, tithes, etc. Covering all the needs of men of God is also a way to worship God. The king had decreed that all of Ezra's needs, as well as the needs of his people, be covered, but he gave clear instructions that the needs of the house of the Lord came first. It has always been true that our first order of service is to seek first the kingdom of God and His righteousness.

Many times we don't see financial progress in our lives because we are not complying with God's needs first. Part of our calling is to become good stewards of everything He places in our hands. The needs of the orphans and widows are not covered by prayer. There are needs that God's children must cover within the faith community and in the neighborhoods where we live. As Jesus says in Luke 10:7, ". . .the workman is worthy of his hire."

We can pray for those who are hungry, but we must also provide bread to meet their physical needs. As James, the Lord's brother tells us, "Suppose you see a brother or sister who has no food or clothing, and you say, 'Good-bye and have a good day; stay warm and eat well'-—but then you don't give that person any food or clothing. What good does that do?" (James 2:15-16)

In the same way, we must support God's projects and ministries. That is living in community and it is also a sign of revival. Unfortunately, there are still many children of God who have not yet understood this revelation. That is why God continues to call to the altar those people who still have areas in their lives they haven't surrendered.

If Jesus were to come to you and ask you to show him your bank account, would you do it without hesitation? Remember, He already knows your spending habits anyway.

Or suppose you lived under a dictatorship where Christianity was outlawed--where you could be imprisoned for involvement in evangelism or any other Christian activity. How would you feel if the government demanded to go through your financial records? Would they find enough evidence to convict you of being a Christian? If you haven't already done so, I urge you to put your finances on the altar. Our spending must reflect our faith. After all, everything we have came from God. Actually, He owns it. We are just using it for this short time He gives us upon the earth. When we give an offering to God, we are really giving Him back something that is already His.

It's like when your small child asks you for a few dollars to buy you a birthday present. The child wants to show his or her love for you, but wouldn't have any way to buy you a gift without the money you provided. The gift is from the child, but the money that purchased it actually came from you. The money we give to God is only there because He blessed us with it. God has blessed us, not only because He loves us, but because He wants us to bless others in His name!

Bringing order back to Judah

Another responsibility that God gave Ezra was to establish authority among His people by appointing and anointing people to be teachers and judges. I admit that there is a great deal of difference between ancient Judah and the modern United States of America. Judah was a theocracy, meaning that the nation's laws were the same as God's laws. The United States is a democracy, and although the nation is founded on Judeo-Christian principles, not all Americans are Christians, or even believers.

Having said that, it is still possible for us to help elect people to office who love the Lord and are guided by Christian principles. We need to vote for men and women who are honest, trustworthy, and truly believe in serving others. Jesus said that anyone who wants to be the leader of all must be the servant of all. (Matthew 20:26)

How can we know who to vote for? We must pray about it and keep our eyes and ears open. Right now, there are people among us whom the Lord has appointed to be leaders for this generation and the next. We don't know their names. They may be in high school right now, or even younger, but the call of God is upon them. God's timing is perfect and He will move whatever He needs to move so these leaders of tomorrow can be ready to serve exactly when they are needed. He is counting on us to "appoint" them as godly leaders in our communities, states and nation.

Another group of people who are living among us right now are those who will serve as future leaders of the church. They are tomorrow's pastors, evangelists, prophets, missionaries, elders, deacons, and other church leaders. It brings a lump to my throat to think of the millions of souls they will win for God's kingdom. It's up to us to encourage them, nurture them, teach them, and—in short—give them everything they need to fulfill the calling God has placed on them. We can provide them with the weapons and tools they need to crash down the gates of hell and set the captives free.

Lesson #9 from the Book of Ezra

Among his many fine qualities, Ezra was a powerful teacher. The Bible says, "For Ezra had set his heart to study the Law of the Lord, and to do it and to teach his statutes and rules in Israel." (Ezra 7:10). As believers in Christ we are all called to teach His truths. As Paul wrote to Timothy, "And so I solemnly urge you before God and before Christ Jesus--who will someday judge the living and the dead when he appears to set up his Kingdom--to preach the Word of God urgently at all times, whenever you get the chance, in season and out, when it is convenient and when it is not. (1 Timothy 4:1-2) Even those who are new in the faith can teach the basic truths and help people under-stand how they can be saved. We must be ready to respond to the teaching opportunities God places before us every day, obeying these words from the Apostle Peter: "Quietly trust yourself to Christ your Lord, and if anybody asks why you believe as you do, be ready to tell him, and do it in a gentle and respectful way." (1 Peter 3:15) Amen.

QUESTIONS FOR SPIRITUAL REFLECTION

1. Talk about some times where God has given you advantage in certain areas so that you are favored.

2. When was the last time you gathered with friends to discuss the Word of God?

3. How have you connected to the leadership calling God has placed on your heart?

4. What can you do to share the gospel with others through service to them?

____

____

____

5. Are you satisfied with the amount of money you give to God's kingdom? If not, how will you change your giving habits?

____

____

____

10

PROCLAIM YOUR FAST

And there by the Ahava Canal, I gave orders for all of us to fast and humble ourselves before our God. We prayed that he would give us a safe journey and protect us, our children, and our goods as we traveled. . . So we fasted and earnestly prayed that our God would take care of us, and he heard our prayer. (Ezra 8:21,23)

As WE CONTINUE TO FOLLOW THE JOURNEY OF THE people of Israel through the book of Ezra, we witness the small and grand gestures of God over His children. We see heavenly purposes within earthly assignments. We can see how different men and women have been called at different times to stand in favor of God's people.

Perhaps you have sometimes wondered if you have a special purpose to fulfill here on earth.

I believe you do.

In fact, I believe that every person who has ever lived, or ever will live, has been tasked with something extremely important to do, just as Ezra was given the job of restoring proper worship and order to the nation of Judah. That doesn't mean everyone carries out the tasks that has been assigned them. Millions of people around the world turn their backs on God and never consider what He might want them to do.

The special purpose you have been given may not seem as important as what Ezra did—transforming an entire nation. But when you get to heaven, you may find that it was just as important in God's eyes. You may have been tasked with saying the right word at the right time that gave someone hope and prevented them from committing an act of violence. You may have planted the seeds of faith that sprouted in someone's heart and caused him or her to be a great evangelist or missionary. Great acts are not always obvious when they happen.

It could be that you are chosen to proclaim a fast in favor of others, a city, or even a nation. It is extremely important to have the correct people in place to accomplish God's will.

When Ezra was on his way toward Jerusalem, he made a stop near the river. As he observed the people who had chosen to go back to Judah with him, he noticed there weren't any Levites among them. Immediately, he appointed wise leaders and sent them to Iddo, the leader of Casiphia, to request servers.

Why were the servers so important? In order to maintain the correct order for the sacrifices in the Temple, it was necessary to have people in specific positions with preassigned responsibilities. This is why when the book of Ezra says: "When the builders completed the foundation of the LORD's Temple, the priests put on their robes and took their places to blow their trumpets. And the Levites, descendants of Asaph, clashed their cymbals to praise the LORD, just as King David had prescribed" (Ezra 3:10).

"There was a perfect order for service so that everything would be done with excellence. The servers were a key element for the order in the service, and Ezra knew this.

What a blessing it is to have people around us who are wise and also have a servant's heart. Serving others is one of the most amazing callings. These are people who always make sure that others are fine, ensure that everyone has eaten, are attentive to the needs in the community, and are loved by all.

A person with a heart of service makes an excellent deacon in a church. They encourage new believers and see that their needs are being met, are excellent as teachers for children and youth, and many times are the people who maintain the Temple in optimum condition.

Most of the servers in the Temple did their work out of love. These people, who were appointed by Ezra, completed the group that would enter with him into Jerusalem. The Temple had been restored and all the bases were established; now it was a matter of seeing that everything was under the correct order established by God and the law of Moses.

Where were the Levites?

God's hand was clearly upon Ezra and those who traveled with him from Babylon to Jerusalem. God blessed and watched over them every step of the way. I'm afraid that those of us who live in the 21st Century A.D don't understand what an arduous journey this was. Remember, these people didn't have cars, motorcycles, bicycles or even roller skates! For the most part, they were on foot. There were no fast-food restaurants or rest areas along the way where they could get a hamburger and soda. There were no road signs to let them know they were on the right road nor Highway Patrolmen to help those who ran into trouble. There were dangers everywhere, but the people relied on the Lord their God and he got them safely through.

Still, there was at least one major disappointment that Ezra had to deal with: Not one Levite "signed up" for the trip. (Ezra 8:15)

Remember that the Levites were the Chosen of the Chosen People. They were set apart to direct the worship in the House of God. Where were they?

The Bible doesn't tell us. Most likely they were busy with their duties, tending to their flock in Babylonia. But undoubtedly, some of them were so busy that they hadn't really taken time to listen to God's voice, to sit before Him and see what He wanted them to do. They were not bad men. The fact that they didn't sign up to go with Ezra doesn't mean they didn't love God. They were serving Him there in the land where their families had lived for 70 years.

And yet, it seems to me that the work Ezra was doing was so important that he should have had more than enough men volunteering to go with him. He should have had to say, "I'm sorry, brothers, but I can't take you all. Some of you will have to stay in Babylonia." But instead, he didn't have a single Levite volunteer and had to send a delegation to Iddo, the leader of the Levites at Casiphia, "to ask him and his relatives and the Temple servants to send us ministers for the Temple of God at Jerusalem." After making this request, Ezra quickly got the men he needed.

I don't want to make too big of an issue about the missing Levites. After all, the Bible doesn't. But I do think there's an important lesson to be learned here, and that is that no human being is infallible, and that includes pastors and leaders in the church. We sometimes make mistakes. We make wrong decisions. We run into trouble when we expect our clergy to be perfect, because only God is perfect. Should we hold our preachers, teachers and other leaders to a higher standard? Absolutely! But always remember, pastors need grace, too. . . and keep your eyes on God. He will never let you down.

Ezra's Fast

Now that the group that was traveling to Jerusalem was complete, Ezra proclaimed a fast before continuing on the way.

> *And there by the Ahava Canal, I gave orders for all of us to fast and humble ourselves before our God. We prayed that he would give us a safe journey and protect us, our children, and our goods as we traveled. For I was ashamed to ask the king for soldiers and horsemen to accompany us and protect us from enemies along the way. After all, we had told the king, "Our God's hand of protection is on all who worship him, but his fierce anger rages against those who abandon him." So we fasted and earnestly prayed that*

our God would take care of us, and he heard our
prayer.(Ezra 8:21-23)

Measured by the words we confess

Ezra knew that those who trust the Lord receive His protection. It was the moment to model what he had preached to God's people: the importance of prayer and fasting, and of being grateful for the Father's protection. He told King Artaxerxes he was certain that God would protect them on their path.

In the same way, we are all measured by the words we confess and profess. We will be labeled as hypocrites if we say we trust God but demonstrate the opposite through our actions. Many times we say one thing but do another. In other words, our words don't sync up with our actions. It's vitally important that we not only believe *in* God, but believe God. If He tells us something, we must take it to heart and really believe it. For the majority of believers, the problem has never been about believing in God's existence; the challenge has been believing in His promises and continuing to trust that if He said it, He will do it, even if our eyes have not yet seen it.

I'm reminded of these challenging words from the book of James 2:19: "You say you have faith, for you believe that there is one God. Good for you! Even the demons believe this, and they tremble in terror." Belief goes much deeper than just acknowledging God's existence. It is an unwavering faith in His goodness and His promises.

It's possible that those who decided to return to Jerusalem with Ezra were fully aware of the dangers they were facing, but they trusted God. So, even though the path toward Jerusalem was full of dangers and Ezra was counting on God's protection, he resorted to one of our most powerful weapons: fasting.

Fasting is one of the spiritual disciplines taught in the Bible. Jesus expects His followers to fast and said that God rewards fasting.

What is fasting? It is reducing or eliminating all food intake, or other pleasures, voluntarily for a determined amount of time and purpose. In the Bible, fasting is always connected with prayer. Fasting can release God's supernatural power. It is a weapon we can use when there is opposition to God's will. Satan loves to cause division, discomfort, fear and defeat. God can use prayer and fasting to give His children victory over the devil.

If you are facing trials or challenges, then the Ezra fast is definitely something you should try. Running from your problems won't work. Victory is obtained by confronting them head on with the guidance and help of the Holy Spirit. Fasting will not make your problems disappear, nor will it magically resolve your problems, but we can see from Ezra's experience that God will provide a solution when you seek Him through prayer and fasting.

Ezra was facing a huge challenge, and he needed God to protect him and everything and everyone who was with him. He had to deliver the materials needed to finish restoring the Temple, which included 7,500 pounds of gold and 25 tons of silver. You can imagine the target these travelers represented. There were hundreds of thieves along the way, just waiting to pull off the crime of the century. As I write these words, the price of gold is just under $2,000 per ounce.

That means an entire pound of gold is worth $32,000, and the gold Ezra's group was transporting would have a total value of $24 million in today's money. Add the 25 tons of silver (estimated value $19.2 million) and you can see what a tempting target they were.

Ezra 8:23 says: "So we fasted and earnestly prayed that our God would take care of us, and He heard our prayer." God not only heard their prayer. He gave them an answer. He told them where they needed to go and what they needed to say. He went into the details of how to hide the gold and silver from those who wanted to steal everything.

When you fast and pray, God will provide step by step solutions to problems you can't solve yourself. God will help you through tough trials in your life. Again, you do not pray and fast to escape problems but to find a solution.

Ezra and his people fasted for two specific things: knowledge and protection. They were praying for these things, not just for themselves but for their children and resources as well, and God answered. God saved all of their resources. He protected them from thieves and instructed them how to hide their precious cargo.

When you fast and pray, the problem might not disappear, but you will see it through God's eyes, and that is an important step toward overcoming it. It is an amazing thing when God allows you to see your trials through His eyes and provides the path to a solution.

Fasting and the United States

In the early days of the United States, when the brand-new country was just beginning to take its place among the world's nations, President John Adams ordered that a day of fasting be set aside. On March 6, 1799, the second president of the United States issued the following proclamation:

> *As no truth is more clearly taught in the Volume of Inspiration, nor any more fully demonstrated by the experience of all ages, than that a deep sense and a due acknowledgment of the growing providence of a Supreme Being and of the*

*accountableness of men to Him as the searcher
of hearts and righteous distributer of rewards
and punishments are conducive equally to the
happiness of individuals and to the well-being
of communities…*

*I have thought proper to recommend, and I
hereby recommend accordingly, that Thursday,
the twenty-fifth day of April next, be observed
throughout the United States of America as a
day of solemn humiliation, fasting, and prayer;*

*That the citizens on that day abstain, as far
as may be, from their secular occupation, and
devote the time to the sacred duties of religion,
in public and in private;*

*That they call to mind our numerous offenses
against the most high God, confess them before
Him with the sincerest penitence, implore his
pardoning mercy, through the Great Mediator
and Redeemer, for our past transgressions, and
that through the grace of His Holy Spirit, we
may be disposed and enabled to yield a more
suitable obedience to his righteous requisitions
in time to come; that He would interpose to
arrest the progress of that impiety and licen-
tiousness in principle and practice so offensive
to Himself and so ruinous to mankind;*

That he would make us deeply sensible that "righteousness exalteth a nation but sin is a reproach to any people" (Proverbs 14:34).

During the Civil War, Abraham Lincoln proclaimed three full days of fasting. In the first of those proclamations, he wrote:

"And I do earnestly recommend to all people, and especially to all ministers and teachers of religion, of all denominations, and to all heads of families to observe and keep that day according to their several creeds and modes of worship in all humility, and with all religious solemnity, to the end that the united prayer of the nation may ascend to the Throne of Grace, and bring down plentiful blessings upon our country."[13]

Wise words indeed from the man widely regarded as the best-ever President of the United States.

What fasting can do

Fasting has a main purpose: getting us closer to God. It's a time we dedicate to prayer and communion with the Father. We subject our bodies into obedience and withhold from certain things to give way for God to come

---

[13] Presidency.ucsb.edu, "Proclamation 85, Proclaiming Day of National Humiliation, Prayer and Fastingm by Gerhard Peters and John T Woolley

close to us. We must understand that fasting is voluntary, and it's a key to strengthen our spiritual lives. It's one of the best tools to get to know God, and we have stopped promoting it. However, there are still many congregations that do twenty-one days of fasting. They pray and fast together as a community. Nevertheless, not all believers implement it as an everyday tool. It's not being taught enough.

The Bible includes many examples of victories that came through fasting and prayer. One of these is found in the 20th chapter of 2 Chronicles, when the armies of the Moabites, Ammonites and the Meunites declared war on Judah. King Jehoshaphat of Judah was terrified when he heard that a vast army was marching his way. His response to the threat was to order everyone in Judah to begin fasting. The Bible says that people from all the towns of Judah came to Jerusalem to seek the Lord's help.

> *Jehoshaphat stood before the community of Judah and Jerusalem in front of the new courtyard at the Temple of the LORD. He prayed, "O LORD, God of our ancestors, you alone are the God who is in heaven. You are ruler of all the kingdoms of the earth. You are powerful and mighty; no one can stand against you! O our God, did you not drive out those who lived in this land when your people Israel arrived? And did you not give this land forever to the descendants of your friend Abraham? Your people settled here*

and built this Temple to honor your name. They said, 'Whenever we are faced with any calamity such as war, plague, or famine, we can come to stand in your presence before this Temple where your name is honored. We can cry out to you to save us, and you will hear us and rescue us.'
"And now see what the armies of Ammon, Moab, and Mount Seir are doing. You would not let our ancestors invade those nations when Israel left Egypt, so they went around them and did not destroy them. Now see how they reward us! For they have come to throw us out of your land, which you gave us as an inheritance. O our God, won't you stop them? We are powerless against this mighty army that is about to attack us. We do not know what to do, but we are looking to you for help" (2 Chronicles 20:5-12).

The Bible says that as the people of Judah stood before the Lord, the Spirit of the Lord came upon one of the men.

He said, "Listen, all you people of Judah and Jerusalem! Listen, King Jehoshaphat! This is what the LORD says: Do not be afraid! Don't be discouraged by this mighty army, for the battle is not yours, but God's. Tomorrow, march out against them. You will find them coming up through the ascent of Ziz at the end of the valley that opens into the wilderness of Jeruel. But you will not even need to fight. Take your positions;

then stand still and watch the Lord's victory. He is with you, O people of Judah and Jerusalem. Do not be afraid or discouraged. Go out against them tomorrow, for the Lord is with you!"

Then King Jehoshaphat bowed low with his face to the ground. And all the people of Judah and Jerusalem did the same, worshiping the Lord. . . . Early the next morning the army of Judah went out into the wilderness of Tekoa. On the way Jehoshaphat stopped and said, "Listen to me, all you people of Judah and Jerusalem! Believe in the Lord your God, and you will be able to stand firm. Believe in his prophets, and you will succeed."

After consulting the people, the king appointed singers to walk ahead of the army, singing to the Lord and praising him for his holy splendor. This is what they sang: "Give thanks to the Lord; his faithful love endures forever!"

At the very moment they began to sing and give praise, the Lord caused the armies of Ammon, Moab, and Mount Seir to start fighting among themselves. The armies of Moab and Ammon turned against their allies from Mount Seir and killed every one of them. After they had destroyed the army of Seir, they began attacking each other. So when the army of Judah arrived

*at the lookout point in the wilderness, all they
saw were dead bodies lying on the ground as far
as they could see. Not a single one of the enemy
had escaped.*

*King Jehoshaphat and his men went out to
gather the plunder. They found vast amounts
of equipment, clothing, and other valuables—
more than they could carry. There was so much
plunder that it took them three days just to col-
lect it all! On the fourth day they gathered in
the Valley of Blessing, which got its name that
day because the people praised and thanked
the LORD there. It is still called the Valley of
Blessing today. (2 Chronicles 20:15-26)*

The Bible is full of stories about people who have
sought the Lord through fasting and prayer.

When Nehemiah heard that much of Jerusalem had
been destroyed, he immediately began to fast and pray
for the holy city's reconstruction:

*"O LORD, God of heaven," he prayed, "the great
and awesome God who keeps his covenant of
unfailing love with those who love him and obey
his commands, listen to my prayer! Look down
and see me praying night and day for your people
Israel. I confess that we have sinned against you.
Yes, even my own family and I have sinned! We*

*have sinned terribly by not obeying the com-
mands, decrees, and regulations that you gave
us through your servant Moses.*

*"Please remember what you told your servant
Moses: 'If you are unfaithful to me, I will scatter
you among the nations. But if you return to me
and obey my commands and live by them, then
even if you are exiled to the ends of the earth, I
will bring you back to the place I have chosen
for my name to be honored'" (Nehemiah 1:5-9).*

Esther, Mordecai and the Jews throughout Persia fasted upon hearing news of Haman's plot to exterminate them (Esther 4:3). Queen Esther did a complete fast before presenting herself in front of the king to ask for mercy for her people, and she asked all of her people to join her: "Go and gather together all the Jews of Susa and fast for me. Do not eat or drink for three days, night or day. My maids and I will do the same. And then, though it is against the law, I will go in to see the king. If I must die, I must die" (Esther 4:16).

Esther fasted for God's coverage and protection. She received grace and favor and was the intermediary for the benefit of God's people.

Daniel also practiced different types of fasting. One of these was not eating certain foods, and the other was when he refused to use perfume for three weeks (Dan.

10:2–3). You may remember that Daniel and his young friends were chosen to take part in a special training program set up by the king. Nebuchadnezzar's plan was to train them for three years, and then bring them into the royal service.

Daniel and his friends were offered the same food and wine that was provided for King Nebuchadnezzar. But they turned it down because they were afraid that it might defile them. They had no idea whether the food they were offered would contradict any of the dietary laws that were handed down by Moses, but they weren't willing to take any chances.

After ten days of eating only vegetables and water, Daniel and his three friends were found to be healthier than the other young men who were enjoying food fit for a king on a regular basis. (Daniel 1:15) Their "fast" had not hurt them, but rather made them stronger.

Finally, remember that after he was baptized by his cousin John the Baptist, Jesus went into the wilderness where He fasted for 40 days and nights. In what must be a bit of an understatement, the Bible says He "became very hungry." It was during this time that Satan tempted him in various ways, but Jesus fought back with the power of Scripture and defeated him.

If Jesus thought fasting was so important that He kept at it for 40 days, then surely it is just as important for those of us who follow Him. There are many spiritual benefits that come through fasting. Your spirit is strengthened. Your relationship with God becomes more solid. The lies the enemy uses against you are shattered. You make a deep dive into the spiritual dimensions, and you develop a new love language with God.

- Furthermore, fasting is a biblical way to humble yourself before God. King David said, "I humbled myself with fasting" (Psalm 35:13, NIV).

- Fasting enables the Holy Spirit to reveal your true spiritual condition, resulting in brokenness, repentance and a transformed life.

- Your confidence and faith in God will be strengthened. You will feel mentally, spiritually and physically refreshed.

Getting to know God better

In the natural world, the closer you become to a person, the more you know them. You get to know how they do things, how they think, and how their hearts work. The same happens in the spiritual realm. As you get closer to God you will develop the capability to distinguish His voice, His desires, and the will He has for your life. In the sixth chapter of Matthew, Jesus has this to say about fasting:

"And when you fast, don't make it obvious, as the hypocrites do, for they try to look miserable and disheveled so people will admire them for their fasting. I tell you the truth, that is the only reward they will ever get. But when you fast, comb your hair and wash your face. Then no one will notice that you are fasting, except your Father, who knows what you do in private. And your Father, who sees everything, will reward you" (Matthew 6:16-18).

I find it really interesting how often Jesus talks about the importance of having the proper motives in everything we do. Fasting is a good thing – unless it is done for the wrong reason, which is to get people to think we are more spiritual than we really are. And what could be more important than prayer--talking to God, listening to His voice and getting to know Him better. And yet Jesus had harsh words for those who pray lofty, eloquent prayers because they want people to say, "That was a beautiful prayer!" Their minds and hearts aren't really on God at all, and so their "beautiful" prayers are blasphemous.

Giving is also a beautiful means of worshiping God. But the Book of Acts tells the story of Ananias and Saphira, who sold some property and gave part of the proceeds to the local church. But then they lied and said that they were giving their entire profit to the church. Their motive wasn't really to support the ministry of the church, but to get the praises of men – and they paid with their lives. (Acts 5:1-11)

It is so important to guard our hearts and double-check our motives, to make sure our actions are intended to honor God.

Rediscovering fasting

Unfortunately, for the most part, fasting as a tool to get closer to God has been lost. We see people using it to bring about miracles and to obtain material blessings. It's as if they regard magic as some kind of magic. The time we spend fasting should be centered on God, not ourselves. All the attention and worship should be focused on the Father.

When you are focusing on Him, all of your spirit, soul, and body receives spiritual nutrients and balm. This makes it easier for you to withstand the enemy's attacks and temptations. As Isaiah 26:3 says, "You will keep in perfect peace all who trust in you, all whose thoughts are fixed on you!"

Fasting is not a "magical" way to get what you want from God, although I have heard teachings that make it seem this is so. As with many other spiritual matters, our motivation is of the utmost importance. We fast because we love God and we want to draw closer to Him. We fast because drawing closer to God will improve our prayer life, and when our prayers are in accordance with God's will they are more powerful and effective.

I believe that God longs to give His people miracles of healing, financial blessing, restoration of marriages and family relationships, and much, much more. But we must not try to manipulate Him or find a sure-fire formula to get what we want from Him. After all, He is God and we are His servants, and not the other way around. Ironically, it is when we take our eyes off of ourselves and focus on Him that He pours out blessings upon us.

I have personally seen the benefits of prayer and fasting many times in my own life, and in the lives of my brothers and sisters in God's family. I remember in particular one dear woman who felt as if she had lost touch with God. For some reason, the closeness she had always experienced with Him had disappeared. She decided to seek the Lord by traveling out to a small community in a remote area where she could spend time alone in her room with the Lord, fasting and seeking him in prayer. Four days went by and nothing happened. Then, on the fifth day, as she was praying, she felt a stirring in her soul.

She opened her eyes and saw that her room was filled with a rosy, pink glow.

"I knew the walls were blue, not pink," she said, "so I closed my eyes and opened them again. The pink glow was still there. It was real."

She also knew immediately that the glow in her room was a sign of God's presence. She could feel Him again. Where had He been? Right there, where He always is. But as sometimes happens, something had closed off the lines of communication. Fasting and prayer had opened them up again.

Yes, there is power in fasting and prayer. This is why Ezra made the people humble themselves and fast as they entered into the presence of God. "So we fasted and earnestly prayed that our God would take care of us, and he heard our prayer." *(Ezra 8:23)* It is amazing to think that they were able to arrive at Jerusalem without one person being injured. This was only because God protected them the entire way. The Word says that God heard and answered all of their prayers because of the fast they carried out.

We all have to face different trials and challenges in life, and we will need to use the tools that take us closer to God.

The only way we can get to know the Father's heart better is by spending time dedicated to Him. Fasting voluntarily is also a sign of revival. It's one of the best ways to reconstruct our altars and our relationship with God. If it weren't a key tool, it would not be mentioned so many times in the Bible.

Matthew 6:17–18 says: *"When you go without food you can pray better, put oil on your head and wash your face. Then nobody knows you are going without food. Then your Father Who sees in secret will reward you."* Did you see it? God not only listens but also sees us. We have His full attention. Fasting is a great way to show God that He is first and more important than anything else in life.

When you fast, God will ordain your steps and give you victory.

Lesson #10 from the Book of Ezra

When we hear people talk about fasting, most of us think of going without food. But a fast can be going without anything that you consider to be an important part of your life. Here's an idea for a fast that can benefit your entire family. Why not try a "media fast" one night per week. This means no radio, television, or reading of newspapers or news magazines. How about cell phones? That's something for you and your family decide, but I suggest you tell your friends and relatives that you will not answer calls on your chosen night. (You may come up with a system for receiving urgent calls.) Taking a media fast will provide your family with an opportunity to read together (especially the Bible), pray together and play wholesome board games together. It will give you and your family an opportunity to get to know each other better, and to draw closer to God.

GUIDE QUESTIONS FOR SPIRITUAL REFLECTION

1. Do you use fasting as a tool to get closer to God?

2. Do you make fasting a regular spiritual discipline? If so, how often do you fast? Weekly? Monthly?

3. How have you benefitted from these special times of fasting? How have they drawn you closer to God?

4. When you have been separated from God, how have you seen His response in your life?

____

____

____

5. What other spiritual tools do you use as part of your intimacy with God?

____

____

____

11

THE RIGHTEOUS PRAYER

"At the time of the sacrifice, I stood up from where I had sat in mourning with my clothes torn. I fell to my knees and lifted my hands to the LORD my God" (Ezra 9:5).

YOU HAVE PROBABLY HEARD THE FAMOUS DEFINI-tion of "insanity," which says that it is doing the same thing over and over again and expecting different results. Although this definition is often attributed to the great physicist Albert Einstein, there is actually no proof that the words came from him. But whoever said this was pretty smart!

Insanity is also what we find in the ninth chapter of the book of Ezra. Once Ezra and his leaders arrived in Jerusalem, they observed that the people of God had, once again, sinned against God and His statutes. As Ezra wrote:

> *When these things had been done, the Jewish leaders came to me and said, "Many of the people of Israel, and even some of the priests and Levites, have not kept themselves separate from the other peoples living in the land. They have taken up the detestable practices of the Canaanites, Hittites, Perizzites, Jebusites, Ammonites, Moabites, Egyptians, and Amorites. For the men of Israel have married women from these people and have taken them as wives for their sons. So the holy race has become polluted by these mixed marriages. Worse yet, the leaders and officials have led the way in this outrage"* (Ezra 9:1–2).

Once again, they were repeating the behaviors that had caused them to live through seventy years of captivity in Babylonia. The people of Israel had ignored God's demand that they not intermingle with the heathen races who lived In the Middle East at that time. Not only were they intermarrying with these tribes, but they were also mixing their religious myths into the truths that Moses had taught them.

It's mind-blowing to read through the story of the Children of Israel and see how they continued to repeat the same mistakes over and over again. They did not sin because of ignorance or by not having the knowledge. They were very aware of the mistakes they were making, but they continued to repeat them. Through it all, God tried desperately to get their attention, but they refused to listen. They would repent and seek to live in accordance with God's laws for a while--sometimes a very short while--and then they would fall back into sin and disobedience.

I recently saw a video that drove home this point to me. The video featured a shepherd who was tending sheep over a rugged patch of ground in the modern-day Middle East. One rambunctious lamb wasn't doing a very good job of watching where he was going and fell into a narrow trench that must have been about four feet deep. No matter how much he squirmed and wriggled, he could not climb out of that trench. He was completely trapped!

But here came the shepherd to the rescue. It wasn't easy, but he managed to get that lamb out of the trench and set him down on safe ground. The animal was so happy to be free, he took off running. And guess what? He hadn't taken more than four or five steps when he tumbled into another trench. The shepherd was exasperated, of course. But he also had compassion for the sheep, and again, stepped in to rescue it. How very much like Jesus, our Good Shepherd.

This illustrates the mercy and grace our Savior has shown, both toward Israel as a nation, and toward you and me as individual Christians. We may stumble again and again because we're not carefully following the "path of righteousness," but He is always ready to rescue us.

When Ezra heard the news about how the Children of Israel were behaving, his heart was shattered. His pain and frustration were evident. As stated in the Word, he tore his clothes, pulled his hair out of his head and beard, and sat on the ground confused and angry. How was it possible that his people would be given a chance to live in freedom and be restored as a people, and then go right back into the behavior that had provoked God's fury and led them into seventy years of captivity? It seemed crazy. They had not learned anything from their past mistakes.

I wonder how many of us see the same sort of conduct in our own lives? Have we also fallen into doing the same things we have always done, but expecting God to do something different? My opinion is that we have. For some reason, we seem not to learn from our mistakes. Many of God's children continue to fight against the same giants, the same trials, return to the same circumstances, and they seem to forget the price they had to pay and the things they had to face because of their sins.

As the Apostle Peter writes in 2 Peter 2:20-22, "*And when people escape from the wickedness of the world by knowing our Lord and Savior Jesus Christ and then get tangled up and enslaved by sin again, they are worse off than before. It*

*would be better if they had never known the way to righteous-
ness than to know it and then reject the command they were
given to live a holy life. They prove the truth of this proverb:
'A dog returns to its vomit." And another says, 'A washed pig
returns to the mud'."*

Even some of the greatest Bible heroes were guilty
of being deceitful. Abraham said his wife Sarah was his
sister because she was beautiful, and he was afraid that
someone might kill him to steal her away. This story is
told in Genesis 12:11–13: *"As he was approaching the border
of Egypt, Abram said to his wife, Sarai, 'Look, you are a very
beautiful woman. When the Egyptians see you, they will say,
"This is his wife. Let's kill him; then we can have her!" So please
tell them you are my sister. Then they will spare my life and
treat me well because of their interest in you."*

As you probably know, this deceit didn't work out
too well for Abraham or Sarai (whose name would later
be changed to Sarah). The story continues over the next
several verses:

> *And sure enough, when Abram arrived in
> Egypt, everyone noticed Sarai's beauty. When
> the palace officials saw her, they sang her praises
> to Pharaoh, their king, and Sarai was taken into
> his palace. Then Pharaoh gave Abram many
> gifts because of her--sheep, goats, cattle, male
> and female donkeys, male and female servants,
> and camels. But the LORD sent terrible plagues*

upon Pharaoh and his household because of Sarai, Abram's wife. So Pharaoh summoned Abram and accused him sharply. "What have you done to me?" he demanded. "Why didn't you tell me she was your wife? Why did you say, 'She is my sister,' and allow me to take her as my wife? Now then, here is your wife. Take her and get out of here!" (Genesis 12:14-19)

I believe it's only because God was with him that Abraham escaped being killed by Pharoah because of his dishonesty. But Abraham did not learn from his mistake. In Chapter 20 of Genesis we find that he once again lied about Sarah for the same reason. After he told everyone that Sarah was his sister, King Abimelech of Gerar took her for his wife. I'm sure the Lord was frustrated about this. And what about poor Sarah, who must have been beyond aggravated that her husband apparently didn't love her enough to stand up and fight for her.

Fortunately for Abraham, God intervened, and Sarah was rescued from her plight.

Unfortunately, Abraham's sin and curse was transferred onto his son, Isaac, who also placed his wife and himself in danger by lying about their relationship.

When the men who lived there (in Gerar) asked Isaac about his wife, Rebekah, he said, "`She is my sister." He was afraid to say, "She is my *wife." He thought, "They will kill me to get her, because she is so beautiful." But some time later, Abimelech, king of the Philistines, looked out his window and saw Isaac caressing Rebekah.*

Immediately, Abimelech called for Isaac and exclaimed, "She is obviously your wife! Why did you say, 'She is my sister'?"

"Because I was afraid someone would kill me to get her from me," Isaac replied.

"How could you do this to us?" Abimelech exclaimed. "One of my people might easily have taken your wife and slept with her, and you would have made us guilty of great sin" (Genesis 26:6–10).

Both father and son (Abraham and Isaac) used deceit instead of depending on God's protection. Their lies put their wives in danger and could have enticed other men into sin. And, unfortunately, this same conduct was repeated in the third generation, when Jacob deceived his father Isaac in order to steal his brother's blessing. That was his first deceit. For this reason, he was also deceived when he worked seven years to obtain the hand of Rachel in marriage, but was given her sister, Leah, instead.

This is a perfect example of how our ungodly conduct can cause adversity for ourselves and our posterity.

This is exactly what happened to the children of Israel. They weren't capable of avoiding the curses their ancestors repeated. This was a nation that grew up in captivity, far from the promised land, far from the Temple of God, and when they had the chance to return and restore the Temple and change their destiny, they continued to repeat unfortunate patterns from the past.

When he heard about the sins the people had committed, Ezra sat down on the floor very confused and upset. The disappointment in his heart was so strong that the Word says: *"Then all who trembled at the words of the God of Israel came and sat with me because of this outrage committed by the returned exiles. And I sat there utterly appalled until the time of the evening sacrifice"* (Ezra 9:4).

Although many people were sinning, there was still a group of people who obeyed God's commands. These people joined Ezra until the time came to offer afternoon sacrifices to Jehovah.

God chose Ezra to become the protector of the Law and, like Moses before him, an intercessor for the Children of Israel. The priest's heart was broken by the way God's own people had disregarded the commands He had given them. It was as if they were thumbing their noses at Him and daring Him to do something about it. Even so, Ezra knew that a return to purity and obedience would set their feet back on the path of righteousness--just as reading and meditating on the Scriptures will help us keep our eyes on God.

At this time, it was necessary for Ezra to go before God to pray for the sins his fellow Jews had committed. His prayer came from a heart that was sad and ashamed, but one that also knew the patience and mercy of God. This prayer, which is widely regarded as one of the great intercessory prayers of the Bible, is recorded in the ninth chapter of Ezra:

> *"O my God, I am utterly ashamed; I blush to lift up my face to you. For our sins are piled higher than our heads, and our guilt has reached to the heavens. From the days of our ancestors until now, we have been steeped in sin. That is why we and our kings and our priests have been at the mercy of the pagan kings of the land. We have been killed, captured, robbed, and disgraced, just as we are today.*

> *"But now we have been given a brief moment of grace, for the LORD our God has allowed a few of us to survive as a remnant. He has given us security in this holy place. Our God has brightened our eyes and granted us some relief from our slavery. For we were slaves, but in his unfailing love our God did not abandon us in our slavery. Instead, he caused the kings of Persia to treat us favorably. He revived us so we*

could rebuild the Temple of our God and repair its ruins. He has given us a protective wall in Judah and Jerusalem.

"And now, O our God, what can we say after all of this? For once again we have abandoned your commands! Your servants the prophets warned us when they said, 'The land you are entering to possess is totally defiled by the detestable practices of the people living there. From one end to the other, the land is filled with corruption. Don't let your daughters marry their sons! Don't take their daughters as wives for your sons. Don't ever promote the peace and prosperity of those nations. If you follow these instructions, you will be strong and will enjoy the good things the land produces, and you will leave this prosperity to your children forever.'

"Now we are being punished because of our wickedness and our great guilt. But we have actually been punished far less than we deserve, for you, our God, have allowed some of us to survive as a remnant. But even so, we are again breaking your commands and intermarrying with people who do these detestable things. Won't your anger be enough to destroy us, so that even this little remnant no longer survives? O LORD, God of Israel, you are just. We come before you in our guilt as nothing but an escaped remnant,

though in such a condition none of us can stand
in your presence" (Ezra 9:6-15).

Ezra's prayer was a plea for forgiveness and mercy. He acknowledged the sins of the people of God, and he was aware that everything was against them. What is most interesting to me about Ezra's prayer is that he counted himself among the guilty, even though he had not actually taken part in the sinful behavior that was so offensive to God. He didn't try to make excuses for himself or remind the Lord that he was innocent. In this way, Ezra was a type of Christ, who, though sinless, gave Himself as a sacrifice for our sins. This gives us a wonderful insight into Ezra's character. As Jesus said, *"There is no greater love than to lay down one's life for one's friends."* (John 15:13) And Paul added, *"Now, most people would not be willing to die for an upright person, though someone might perhaps be willing to die for a person who is especially good. But God showed his great love for us by sending Christ to die for us while we were still sinners." (Romans 5:7-8)*

This was the kind of love Ezra had for his countrymen. Instead of making excuses, when he prayed, Ezra brought to memory the instructions God had given through His prophets--clear, precise instructions that had been disregarded.

Today, we have the complete Bible, which is our summary of God's expectations, statutes and commandments. We must be careful not to do what the ancient of Israel did, and disregard what God is saying to us through His Holy Word.

Another important thing to note about Ezra's prayer is that it is a shining example of how to enter God's presence to ask for His mercy and forgiveness. The Bible says in Hosea 4:6: *"My people are destroyed for lack of knowledge."* (NIV) So, if we correctly use the Scriptures, we have the full knowledge we need to avoid falling into the enemy's traps.

Proverbs 2:2–5 says:

> *"Tune your ears to wisdom,*
>   *and concentrate on understanding.*
> *Cry out for insight,*
>   *and ask for understanding.*
> *Search for them as you would for silver;*
>   *seek them like hidden treasures.*
> *Then you will understand what it means to*
> *fear the LORD*
>   *and you will gain knowledge of God."*

This chapter is evidence that good intentions alone are not enough to keep us from repeating old habits and straying from God. We must apply God's healing balm to the root of our problems. Having a knowledge of God's laws is not enough to live a life of integrity. After all, we are aware of earthly laws and their legal consequences, and we still have violated some of them--like exceeding the speed limit or burning a U-turn where such a move is prohibited. If you haven't ever broken any laws like these, I salute you. You're a better person than I am.

The same thing occurs with the laws of the kingdom; we know them because we have read them in the Bible, but sometimes we still disobey. The key is to remain in prayer, understand that we are not self-sufficient, and know that we can stand in righteousness before God only because of His favor, grace, and mercy.

Practice intercessory prayer

Like Moses before him, Ezra practiced intercessory prayer on behalf of his Jewish brothers and sisters. You may remember how Moses prayed for the people after they had sinned by worshiping the golden calf:

> *The next day Moses said to the people, "You have committed a terrible sin, but I will go back up to the LORD on the mountain. Perhaps I will be able to obtain forgiveness for your sin."*

> *So Moses returned to the LORD and said, "Oh, what a terrible sin these people have committed. They have made gods of gold for themselves. But now, if you will only forgive their sin -- but if not, erase my name from the record you have written!"*

*But the L**ord** replied to Moses, "No, I will erase
the name of everyone who has sinned against
me. Now go, lead the people to the place I told
you about. Look! My angel will lead the way
before you. And when I come to call the people
to account, I will certainly hold them responsible for their sins" (Exodus 32:30-34).*

What book was Moses talking about? The Book of Life.
In other words, he was willing to give up his own life
so that the Israelites could be forgiven. What amazing
love he showed! The kind of love Christ showed for
all mankind.

Intercession is the prayer that appeals to God for our
needs and the needs of others. But it is so much more than
that. Intercession is embracing God's will and denying
our own so that His can be fulfilled.

Intercession can be a battle, the key to God's plans
for our lives. But the battlefield is not on this earth. The
Bible says: "For we are not fighting against flesh-and-
blood enemies, but against evil rulers and authorities of
the unseen world, against mighty powers in this dark
world, and against evil spirits in the heavenly places"
(Ephesians 6:12).

The man who prayed for 52 years

Intercessory prayer sometimes requires a great deal of patience and perseverance. For some reason, the answers we seek do not always come immediately. I can think of many great men and women who persisted in prayers for years. Without a doubt the greatest example of an intercessory prayer warrior was my Mother. Mom prayed for her children for decades until we all came to Christ. I remember hearing her cry out to God for each of us privately in her prayer room. The spirit would fall powerfully upon her and she in turn would lay hands on us and ask God to reveal himself to us personally. He sure did, today my siblings are all pastors and leaders in the church. God answers prayer!

I read a story of a man named George Muller.[14] As a young man, Muller served time in prison for theft. After turning his life over to Christ, he became one of the most generous men of the 19th century. He is known primarily for his efforts to help orphans, who often lived in horrible poverty in those days, surviving only by stealing, begging or working in brutal conditions in workhouses.

Muller is said to have given more than $700,000 of his own money to this work. Today, that $700,000 would be worth about $35 million.

---

[14] William J. Petersen and Randy Petersen, "100 Amazing Answers to Prayer," Pages 129-130

There is much more I could say about George Muller. But right now I want to focus on his amazing efforts as an intercessory prayer warrior. Like Ezra and Moses, who prayed valiantly for their people, Muller spent 52 years praying for the salvation of a group of men he knew. I'm not saying that he spent every minute of that time in prayer. Of course not. But he prayed long and hard for these people, and he never gave up. I wonder how many of us would persevere in prayer for over five decades.

Muller kept careful records of the prayers he prayed and the dates God answered them. He estimated that more than 50,000 of his requests had been answered during his lifetime. Most of these were for necessities for people in need, such as life-sustaining food for the orphans in his care. But his prayers for salvation for his friends did not bring quick answers. Here's how Muller told it:

> *"In November, 1844, I began to pray earnestly for the conversion of five individuals. I prayed every day without a single intermission. . . . Eighteen months elapsed before the first of the five was converted. I thanked God and prayed on for the others. Five years lapsed, and then the second was converted. I thanked God for the second, and prayed on for the other three. Day by day I continued to pray for them, and six years passed before the third was converted.*

"I thanked God for the three and went on praying for the other two. These men remain unconverted. The man to whom God, in the riches of His grace has given tens of thousands of answers to prayer in the self-same hour or day in which they were offered has been praying day by day for nearly thirty-six years for the conversion of these individuals, and yet they remain unconverted. But I hope in God, I pray on, and look yet for the answer. They are not converted yet, but they will be."

When Muller died in 1898, neither one of the men he prayed for had professed faith in Christ. But two years later, both of them accepted Him as Lord and Savior. Muller's prayers were answered!

Intercessory prayer has a special place in the spiritual world. It gives us the winning edge in the battles we face every day. This is where the battles of our own lives, our families, our friends, and our nation are won or lost. Through intercessory prayer you can enter into God's presence and discover His plans for the situation you are facing. I believe that God wants us all to be intercessors--for our families, our friends, our brothers and sisters in Christ, our communities and our nation – and for anyone else He puts on our hearts.

Since prayer alone is not enough, you need an objective for your prayers! To discover God's plans for you, all you have to do is ask.

The Bible says: "If you need wisdom, ask our generous God, and he will give it to you. He will not rebuke you for asking" (James 1:5). When we ask God for wisdom, His desires become the focus of our prayers. "Don't copy the behavior and customs of this world, but let God transform you into a new person by changing the way you think. Then you will learn to know God's will for you, which is good and pleasing and perfect" (Romans 12:2).

Intercessory prayer is a serious matter. Just like soldiers who are preparing for battle, we can't face our enemies if we leave our weapons behind. We must also recognize that Jesus has complete control of the situation. He is King of Kings and Lord of lords! Intercession is a key weapon of our spiritual warfare that can demolish strongholds in the spiritual world. "We are human, but we don't wage war as humans do. We use God's mighty weapons, not worldly weapons, to knock down the strongholds of human reasoning and to destroy false arguments" (2 Cor. 10:3–4).

The Power of Prayer

Ezra knew there was great power in prayer. He knew because He had seen God respond to numerous prayers, bringing peace, joy and healing into very difficult situations. The same God is still on the throne today, still responding to the prayers of His people, still giving joy for ashes, hope for despair and health for sickness.

Please remember, when you pray, that the effectiveness of your prayer does not depend on the words you use, how articulate you are, or whether you use the right formula. Several years ago, I saw a sign in front of a church that I have never forgotten. It said, "The power of prayer does not depend on the person who's praying, but on the One Who hears the prayer." Like I said, I've always remembered those words, and I hope you will, too. Sometimes, a stammering prayer of a few minutes results in tremendous miracles. As God told the apostle Paul, "My power works best in weakness" (2 Corinthians 12:9).

Paul also writes, in Romans 8:26, "And the Holy Spirit helps us in our weakness. For example, we don't know what God wants us to pray for. But the Holy Spirit prays for us with groanings that cannot be expressed in words."

In their book, "100 Amazing Answers to Prayer," William J. and Randy Petersen present some amazing examples of how God responds to the prayers of His children.[15] For example, Billy Graham told about a missionary who was traveling with his family in a remote and dangerous part of the country where they were serving God. They were trying to make it home by nightfall, but finally

---

[15] Wiliam J. Petersen and Randy Petersen, "100 Amazing Answers to Prayer," Pages 175-177

realized that wasn't going to happen, so they decided to camp out on a hillside. They knew there were dangerous bandits in this area, but the missionary and his family prayed that God would protect them. They slept safely through the night and then returned home.

> *"A few days later, the missionary saw a patient at the Mission hospital who confessed that he belonged to [a] bandit gang. The man recognized the missionary from that hillside and asked about the armed regiment that was guarding his family that night. 'We intended to rob you,' he said, 'but we were afraid of the soldiers you had around you – twenty-seven of them.'*

> *"When the missionary returned home on furlough, he told the story to one of the churches that supported him. Someone consulted the church's records and found they had a prayer meeting that night with twenty-seven people present."*

The Petersens report that Corrie ten Boom also told a story of what happened when rebels planned to attack a missionary school in Africa and kill the 200 or so students and teachers who lived there. Aware that they were in danger, the residents prayed for God's protection.

> *"The rebel army numbered in the hundreds, but when they got close to the school, they suddenly saw something and fled. The same thing*

happened a second night and a third. When one of the rebels was wounded and brought to the Mission hospital, he was asked why they had fled. The answer came: 'We saw hundreds of soldiers in white uniforms, and we became scared.'"

A similar story comes from Indonesia. After two missionaries were killed by cannibals, other missionaries in a nearby area felt that they, too, were threatened and spent hours on their knees in prayer. After this continued for some time, one of the tribesmen came to their compound and asked if he could "have a look" at their watchmen:

"'What watchmen?' asked the missionary. 'I don't have any watchmen.'

"'Oh, yes, you do. You station them around your house at night to protect you.'

"The tribesman wouldn't be convinced until he had searched the missionary's house, looking under the beds and in the closets.

"'We came together to kill you and your wife,' he explained before he left. 'But night after night, when we came near, a double row of watchmen with glittering weapons stood close to your home. . . . We went to a professional assassin, who laughed at us because of our cowardice.'

*But when the assassin came to the missionary's
house, he too saw the watchmen and ran away."*

*"The missionary then got his Bible and showed
the tribesman how God had promised to guard
and defend His children."*

There are so many stories like these three that give proof. . . our God answers prayer!

You are never alone

When spiritual warfare comes to you, as it will, trust that you are not alone. Jesus is with you and He is also intervening in your favor. The Bible says Jesus is capable *"once and forever, to save those who come to God through him. He lives forever to intercede with God on their behalf"* (Hebrews 7:25).

This type of prayer never gives up. It supports all the turnovers and surpasses each obstacle. It's the prayer that continues until we learn God's will in every situation that we face (Philippians 3:12). This type of prayer is needed to see advances in your life and in the lives of those around you.

Throughout the Bible, God is looking for those willing to fight the spiritual battle for His people. God said: *"I looked for someone who might rebuild the wall of righteousness that guards the land. I searched for someone to stand in the gap in the wall so I wouldn't have to destroy the land, but I found no one"* (Ezekiel 22:30). It's through intercession that we can be offensive in spiritual battles.

Jesus said that the gates of hell will not be able to stand against the church.(Matthew 16:18) The picture I get from this is an army of believers moving forward into Satan's territory, rescuing those he has enslaved. We are not to stay forever on the defensive, huddling together in fear and wondering if we can possibly withstand the attacks launched by Satan and his demonic soldiers.

God will heal our land

God promises that when we follow His calling and take our rightful place in the spiritual battle for the hearts and minds of men, He will reach out and heal our land (2 Chronicles 7:14).

Does our land need to be healed? There is no doubt about it. We talked earlier about how depressing it is to watch the news on TV, or read the morning newspaper.

I turned on the news this morning just to see if things are as bad as they were last time I watched, and found that, yes indeed, they are. I managed to watch about 20 minutes, and here are a few of the stories I saw:

An elderly grandmother had been robbed of most of her life-savings by con artists claiming to be her grandson.

They used Artificial Intelligence to mimic his voice, telling her that he had been involved in a car crash and needed several thousand dollars immediately. I was left wondering if there is anything lower than a thief who would steal the life savings of a person who has worked hard all her life and saved what she could. Whatever happened to integrity?

The next story was about another mass shooting, in which four people had died. We have become accustomed to such tragedies, with much higher death tolls. The way the story was presented, four deaths didn't even seem like that big of a deal. What a tragedy that we have seen so many mass shootings that we have become almost numb to them. Whatever happened to believing in the sanctity of human life?

Story Number Three was a report on a woman and her boyfriend who had been convicted for the beating death of her nine-year-old son. Tears came to my eyes as the reporter recounted the story of the child's death. My only comfort came in knowing that God Himself shared my grief, for as Jesus said: *"Beware that you don't look down on any of these little ones. For I tell you that in heaven their angels are always in the presence of my heavenly Father . . . .it is not my heavenly Father's will that even one of these little ones should perish"* (Matthew 18:10,14). Many of us have fought long and hard to protect unborn children, but we must do more to help these children as they grow up.

This is about where I checked out on the morning news, but there are many other reasons why our land needs to be healed. For example:

Millions of Americans are addicted to drugs and alcohol and thousands die every year from taking drugs like Fentanyl. During 2021, the last year for which we have complete records, 106,000 Americans lost their lives to drugs, and that's not counting those who died due to the carelessness of drunk drivers. We need healing from drugs.

We also need healing and protection from natural disasters like tornadoes, hurricanes, floods and wild-fires. All of these have been sweeping across the United States over the last few years, destroying communities and leaving scores of people dead. As I was preparing to write this book, I heard that two major insurance companies have said they can no longer afford to insure new homes in California, due to the danger of wildfires there. It seems apparent to me that God's hand is in this because we have turned away from Him. If we return to Him, he can and will calm the storms and give us peace and protection.

Of course there are other ways our country needs healing. Instead of working together for the good of all, we are divided by hate. Whereas there are important issues, we are not willing to look for common ground. All too often, we are willing to believe the most outrageous lies about men and women who may not see things the way we do. Yes, we must work for decency, morality and godliness. But we cannot please God if we have anger and malice in our hearts. We need to be healed from division and hate.

God is calling His people to became intercessory prayer warriors. He is not seeking people who know how to pray a perfect prayer, but rather hearts that are anxious to see His will done here on earth. My prayer is that we can return to the Lord so that He can give us an interceding heart because, "The earnest prayer of a righteous person has great power and produces wonderful results" (James 5:16).

We've talked before about how God chose Ezra to be an intercessor for the Jewish people. As is always true of God, it seems He made a perfect choice. It's difficult to imagine anyone else having the passion and concern for the Jewish people that Ezra had. His heart was deeply burdened for those who had strayed away from God. He knew that a return to obedience would change everything and restore Judah to its proper status as one of the world's great nations.

Today, a return to studying and following the truths found in the Scriptures will bless us in the same way. When we show that we have a true desire to serve the Lord, it will have a powerful effect on those around us. We can learn so much from this great man of God.

Lesson #11 from the Book of Ezra

Prayer was a vital tool in the work of rebuilding Jerusalem and bringing the city's Jewish inhabitants back to God. Ezra writes, "As I lay on the ground in front of the Temple, weeping and praying and making this confession, a large crowd of men, women, and children gathered around and cried with me." (Ezra 10:1) This was a pivotal moment in the physical and spiritual rebirth of Jerusalem. The Bible has a lot to say about the effectiveness of sincere prayer. Prayers offered up by godly men and women have healed the sick, raised the dead and prevented catastrophes of all types. Prayer absolutely works, so why do we not lean on the power of prayer more often? If you are not spending time with God in prayer every day, I urge you to start doing it right now. And when you do, be sure to take time to listen to what God wants to say to you. After all, prayer isn't a monologue, but a conversation.

QUESTIONS FOR SPIRITUAL REFLECTION

1. Have you ever had to step into the spiritual gap for a person or cause? Explain your answer.

____

____

____

2. Have you ever experienced a time when you were under spiritual attack from the enemy? What steps did you take to withstand his attacks?

____

____

____

3. Are you involved in intercessory prayer for someone or something? If so, what lessons do you learn from the story of George Muller?

____

____

____

4. List some of your Bible verses about prayer:

____

____

____

5. List several of your prayers that were answered by the Lord. (Remembering past victories can give us hope and faith as we face today's battles.)

____

____

____

12

REVIVAL ON EARTH

"Ezra was praying and telling their sins and crying and lying on the ground before the house of God. Many people, men, women, and children, gathered around him from Israel, for the people cried with many tears" **(Ezra 10:1).**

M Y DEAR READER, WE ARE COMING QUICKLY TO the end of our time together. I hope that our study of the Book of Ezra has been as beneficial for you as it has been for me. Every time I read this wonderful book of the Bible, I gain some insight I hadn't noticed before. Of course, this is true of the entire Bible, which is a continuous fount of knowledge and wisdom.

The book of Ezra closes in a very interesting manner. Because of Ezra's prayer and breakdown, many people of Israel--both men and women--joined him and cried bitterly. It was an inspirational moment in which the Holy Ghost stirred the hearts of the children of God to repentance.

Have you ever seen anything like this amazing event that is recorded in the tenth chapter of Ezra? I can't say that I have, but I have seen some that come close to this. There are times when the Holy Spirit moves on the hearts of God's people and everyone breaks into tears. It is a truly amazing and humbling experience to weep with your brothers and sisters in the Lord--to feel their sorrows and to know that they feel yours.

I have been in services where it seemed that people couldn't wait for the altar call to be given so they could run down to the front of the church. This is the Holy Spirit's doing and it is an amazing thing.

But God never leaves us in our sorrow and tears. The same Spirit that gives us godly sorrow also fills our hearts with the joy of salvation and puts laughter in our mouths.

The truth is that any encounter with the Holy Spirit is going to change us in profound ways. Some of us have forgotten how to cry, while others no longer remember how to laugh. Wherever we are, we need the change that only the Holy Spirit can give us.

One of the signs of revival is genuine repentance. Revival is not seeing manifestations of tongues in a service or people dancing in the Spirit. The revival we are waiting on is the return of the children of God to His heart.

True revival begins with a sincere encounter with the Word of God. If this encounter helps us see that we are not living according to God's will, if this comprehension of our sins breaks our hearts and the pain moves us to confess our sin to God, there is still another step we must take. That is the step of repentance.

To repent is to be convicted, to feel sadness and remorse for our actions, and to confess our sins to God. But there is also one more step to take, because all of these things can be present without producing an external, lasting change in our lives. For example, if a person who uses drugs acknowledges that he or she has a problem but isn't willing to take the necessary steps to change their behavior, then they are like those I mentioned in the first chapter: stirred but not awakened to change their lives.

True repentance involves a determination to turn away from your sinful behavior, and thus change the course of your life. It's not just about being aware that you are going in the wrong direction. You must feel bad enough about it that you turn around and head in the right direction. A course correction is needed.

In the middle of Ezra's intercession, hope arose: ". . *.for the people cried with many tears. Then Shecaniah son of Jehiel, a descendant of Elam, said to Ezra, 'We have been unfaithful to our God, for we have married these pagan women of the land. But in spite of this there is hope for Israel. Let us now make a covenant with our God to divorce our pagan wives and to send them away with their children. We will follow the advice given by you and by the others who respect the commands of our God. Let it be done according to the Law of God'"* (Ezra 10:2-4).

This is when the Jews who had returned from Babylonia to Judah felt a need to establish a pact with God, promising to return to His ways. The people knew that Ezra had the responsibility to make sure that they would turn back from their wrong ways and bad decisions, and they were willing to support him and help him with his assignment. Undoubtedly, this was a painful process for many of these people. It meant separating from the foreign women they had married and even the children who had been born to these women.

It is often necessary to sacrifice people, projects, and things that we have clung to even though they have never been in God's plans for us. These aren't necessarily bad things; they might even be things that other people consider to be good, but it is necessary to surrender them to see God's blessing in our lives.

It may seem crazy to believe that there are good things that are outside of God's will for us, but this is a fact. Getting married and establishing a family do not appear to be bad things. On the contrary, having a family is one of God's greatest blessings--unless we ignore His will and marry someone who is not a believer, or someone who is going to stand in the way of our service to God. A Christian should not want to be married to someone who drinks to excess, takes illegal drugs, behaves in an immoral way, or has no interest in the things of God.

During my years as a pastor, I have counseled dozens of women who made the mistake of thinking they could change a man once they married him. Yes, I have counseled a number of men who have made the same mistake--but it seems to be more prevalent among women. They think, "Sure, he drinks a little bit now, but I can get him to change that." Or, "He may have hit me a couple of times, but I know he loves me, and he won't do it anymore." Or, "Yes, he flirts with other women, but that's just because he's still a little immature. I know he'll get over that."

I believe that anyone can be forgiven of their sins, no matter how egregious those sins may be. But I also believe that those who are forgiven must repent and turn away from their wrongdoing. It is folly to marry someone and think, "I'll reform him--or her--later."

A person who has no room for God in his life will never repent. That makes me wonder what would have happened to the Children of Israel if God had not sent people like Ezra, Nehemiah, Jeremiah and others to minister to them.

The Bible warns us that "bad company corrupts good character (1 Corinthians 15:33)" and warns us, "Don't team up with those who are unbelievers. How can righteousness be a partner with wickedness? How can light live with darkness?" (2 Corinthians 6:14)

God's people were called to live in a specific way and conduct themselves under God's laws and commandments. When they got mixed up with the wrong people, they became careless about obeying God's will. This provoked them to worship false gods and idols.

I urge you to ask yourself if there is something you need to give up for God? Is there someone in your life who tempts you to move away from the Lord in some way. Are you drawn to a television show that glorify violence, illicit sex and ungodly living? Do you belong to a club where there is coarse joking and excessive drinking? Whatever it is in your life that stands between you and God – I urge you to give it up!

I once read about a church that built an extra room where people could give up things that were precious to them--so precious in fact that they had come between them and God. The room was filled with items like photograph albums, jewelry, locks of children's hair, and other personal treasures – all of which had been offered up as sacrifices to God. These things weren't worth much in the way of money. But, for some reasons, they had become idols and their owners wanted to give them up to God. Money is important because it provides for preachers, teachers and evangelistic materials. It also can be used to buy time on radio and television for Christian programming, and keep the doors open and the lights turned on in your church.

But I'm sure there are many things in your life that are more important than money, and I hope you will look for innovative ways to share those things with God.

The king who wouldn't repent

There are a number of stories throughout the Bible of people who claimed that they had turned away from their sins, but really refused to let them go and paid a dear price. I think of Pharaoh, for example, who was finally convinced by the power of God to let the Children of Israel leave Egypt--and slavery--behind.

You know the story. When Moses went before the ruler of Egypt and asked him to let God's people go, Pharaoh laughed at him. Exodus 5:1-2 says:

Moses and Aaron went and spoke to Pharaoh.
They told him, "This is what the LORD, *the God*
of Israel, says: Let my people go so they may
hold a festival in my honor in the wilderness."

"Is that so?" retorted Pharaoh. "And who is
the LORD*? Why should I listen to him and let*
Israel go? I don't know the LORD, *and I will not*
let Israel go." (Exodus 5:1-2)

Instead of letting the Israelites go, Pharaoh told his officials to make their work even harder. The first thing he did was to stop providing the straw the Israelites needed for the process of making bricks for the Egyptians. Instead, the Israelites would have to find their own straw, but they were still expected to produce the same number of bricks as before.

After this, God struck Egypt with nine devastating plagues to show His power and convince Pharaoh to set the Israelites free from their chains. Through it all, Pharaoh stood firm. He would not release the Israelites despite plagues of boils, locusts, frogs, hail, etc.

Then came the final, devastating plague, the death of every Egyptian family's first-born sons. When this happened, Pharaoh saw the error of his ways. He repented of his stubborn determination to keep the Jews in slavery at all costs. In fact, he couldn't wait to see them leave the country. Good riddance!

Unfortunately for Pharaoh, and the country of Egypt, almost as soon as the Israelites were on their way out of Egypt, he changed his mind:

> *So Pharaoh harnessed his chariot and called up his troops. He took with him 600 of Egypt's best chariots. . . . As Pharaoh approached, the people of Israel looked up and panicked when they saw the Egyptians overtaking them. They cried out to the LORD, and they said to Moses, "Why did you bring us out here to die in the wilderness? Weren't there enough graves for us in Egypt? What have you done to us? Why did you make us leave Egypt? Didn't we tell you this would happen while we were still in Egypt? We said, "Leave us alone! Let us be slaves to the Egyptians. It's better to be a slave in Egypt than a corpse in the wilderness!"*

> *But Moses told the people, "Don't be afraid. Just stand still and watch the LORD rescue you today. The Egyptians you see today will never be seen again. The LORD himself will fight for you. Just stay calm."*

Just as Moses said He would, the Lord did fight for the Israelites. He parted the waters of the Red Sea, allowing them to walk across on dry land. But when the Egyptians followed, they were not so fortunate.

Then the Egyptians—all of Pharaoh's horses, chariots, and charioteers—chased them into the middle of the sea. But just before dawn the LORD looked down on the Egyptian army from the pillar of fire and cloud, and he threw their forces into total confusion. He twisted their chariot wheels, making their chariots difficult to drive. "Let's get out of here--away from these Israelites!" the Egyptians shouted. "The LORD is fighting for them against Egypt!"

When all the Israelites had reached the other side, the LORD said to Moses, "Raise your hand over the sea again. Then the waters will rush back and cover the Egyptians and their chariots and charioteers." So as the sun began to rise, Moses raised his hand over the sea, and the water rushed back into its usual place. The Egyptians tried to escape, but the LORD swept them into the sea. Then the waters returned and covered all the chariots and charioteers—the entire army of Pharaoh. Of all the Egyptians who had chased the Israelites into the sea, not a single one survived. (Exodus 14:6-7, 10-14, 23-28)

Because Pharaoh refused to repent of his arrogant attitude toward the Lord and his mistreatment of His people, he paid the ultimate price. As Paul says in 2 Corinthians 7:10: *"For the kind of sorrow God wants us to experience leads us away from sin and results in salvation. There's no regret for that kind of sorrow. But worldly sorrow, which lacks repentance, results in spiritual death."*

But consider, on the other hand, the fate of a tax collector named Zacchaeus. His story is found in the 19th chapter of Luke. The Bible doesn't say right out that he was a crook, but it does say that he had become very rich, so we know he probably wasn't the most honest fellow in the world. Like most tax collectors of his day, Zacchaeus was hated by his fellow-Jews. He worked for the Roman government, collecting the exorbitant taxes that went into the treasury of Caesar. Tax collectors like Zacchaeus were seen as traitors and criminals, and not without reason. In addition to collecting the taxes that were required by the Roman government, they were free to keep as much as they could get for themselves, and many of them had become rich this way.

Zacchaeus heard that Jesus was coming to town, and he wanted to see the Master--but he had a problem. He was short, and the streets were crowded with people who also wanted to get a look at the Messiah. Being an industrious man, Zacchaeus had an idea. He would climb a tree where he could get a good look at the Lord as he passed by. So that's exactly what he did. He found a sycamore--a type of fig tree that was common in the Middle East in those days--and was perfect for climbing because it had many low-hanging branches. From here, he had a perfect view of the procession that passed below.

He was shocked when Jesus looked up at him and called him by name: "Zacchaeus, quick! Come down. I must be a guest in your home today." Zacchaeus wasn't the only one who was shocked. Zacchaeus was notorious in Jericho. The people wanted nothing to do with him and they were disappointed that Jesus wanted to be the guest of such a villain.

But the eighth and ninth verses of this chapter report that:

> *Zacchaeus stood before the Lord and said, "I will give half my wealth to the poor, Lord, and if I have cheated people on their taxes, I will give them back four times as much!"*

> *Jesus responded, "Salvation has come to this home today, for this man has shown himself to be a true son of Abraham. For the Son of Man came to seek and save those who are lost."*

Zacchaeus repented and his life was forever changed. He didn't resign from his job, but he resolved that from now on he would treat people fairly, and he would also seek to make restitution for his past wrongs. Zacchaeus is a marvelous example of what repentance can be like and what it can do.

God's representatives on earth

When you create a covenant with the Father, it means surrendering your will and accepting His, believing that His plans for you are much better than the plans you have for yourself. The will of God is for us to be His hands and feet here on earth. Isaiah 42:6–8 says:

> *"I, the* LORD, *have called you to demonstrate*
> *my righteousness.*
> *I will take you by the hand and guard you,*
> *and I will give you to my people, Israel, as a*
> *symbol of my covenant with them.*
> *And you will be a light to guide the nations.*
> *You will open the eyes of the blind.*
> *You will free the captives from prison,*
> *releasing those who sit in dark dungeons.*
> *I am the* LORD; *that is my name!*
> *I will not give my glory to anyone else, nor*
> *share my praise with carved idols."*

That is the heart of God, a heart that desires us to help others walk away from darkness. The problem is that many people have been walking in darkness for so long that they don't recognize the light. They have become accustomed to living without it. This is why it's important for God's people to experience true repentance. The Holy Ghost is touching the hearts of His children to restore the ruins and reignite the flames of passion and belief. The altar is His presence, the fire is His Holy Spirit, and the sacrifice is you.

Jesus is coming soon

Anyone who has his or her eyes open can see that Christ's return is very near. The Bible lists a number of events that will signify that the end of this present age is approaching. I want to touch briefly on five of them.

1) **There will be wars and rumors of wars**. Matthew 24:7 puts it this way: *"Nation will go to war against nation, and kingdom against kingdom."*

   Look at what is happening in Ukraine, where Russian missiles are devastating civilian neighborhoods and killing hundreds of innocent men, women and children. In the midst of all the carnage, Russian president Vladimir Putin threatens to unleash his nuclear arsenal, which would certainly lead to the most devastating war ever and possibly millions of deaths. Fighting also continues in the Middle East, as Israel's enemies launch missile attacks against her, and Israel retaliates with aerial bombardments. These are just two of many conflicts that are taking place around the world. War has been a part of life on this planet for thousands of years. In fact, the Jewish captives in Babylon were there due to war. But the situation seems to be getting much worse instead of better.

2) **There will be earthquakes and other natural disasters.** *"There will be great earthquakes, and there will be famines and plagues in many lands, and there will be terrifying things and great miraculous signs from heaven."* (Luke 21:11)

One can hardly watch the news these days without hearing of a powerful earthquake, a devastating swarm of tornadoes, wildfires burning out of control, or torrential rains that cause floods and landslides. As I have been writing this book, catastrophic wildfires in Canada have sent smoke pouring into the United States, poisoning the air in cities like New York, Philadelphia and Chicago. It almost seems that nature is rebelling against us and the weather has gone crazy. Some people point to climate change as the cause for all of this, but whatever the underlying cause may be, we know that it's all part of God's plan.

3) **Scoffers will be all around us.** Here is what the apostle Peter had to say about this: *"I want to remind you that in the last days scoffers will come, mocking the truth and following their own desires. They will say, 'What happened to the promise that Jesus is coming again? From before the times of our ancestors, everything has remained the same since the world was first created.'"* (2 Peter 3:3-4)

Does this sound familiar to you? It certainly does to me. I can't remember a time when faith was mocked as it is today--in movies, television, books, by stand-up comedians, and in ordinary conversation. It seems to me that there is very little reverence or fear for the things of God. Over the past few years there have been a number of best-selling books that ridiculed belief in God. These include "God is Not Good," by Christopher Hitchens, and "The God Delusion" by Richard Dawkins. We are thumbing our collective noses at God and taking his lack of response as weakness when it is really a sign of His tremendous patience and desire to see everyone saved.

The first three signs we've talked about are negative, but the final two are extremely positive.

4) **The gospel will be preached to all nations.**

Matthew 24:14 says, "*And this gospel of the kingdom will be preached in the whole world as a testimony to all nations, and then the end will come.***"**

Until the developments of the last 100 years, this was not possible. It has only been through breakthroughs in radio, television, and satellite communications that it has become possible to take the gospel into the whole world. Even now, there are people in some remote areas--such as isolated island tribes in the Pacific and Indian oceans, and in northern China, that have not been reached with the gospel. According to an organization called *Finishing the Task,* there are 144 remaining unengaged, unreached people groups numbering over 5.7 million people that are still beyond the reach of the Gospel.[16] But it is only a matter of time until they hear the good news. Finishing the Task, which is headed by Pastor Rick Warren, has set a goal of reaching all the unreached unengaged people groups in the world by 2025. Other organizations such as the American Bible Society and Wycliffe Bible Translators are hard at work, translating the Bible into languages that are only spoken by a few thousand, or a few hundred, people. The prophecy that the gospel will be taken into every nation will be fulfilled any day now!

5) Jews who have been dispersed into countries around the world will return to Israel.

No people on earth have suffered as much the Jews. They have been expelled from countries where they lived for centuries, persecuted in many ways and murdered en masse. Adolf Hitler was not the first person who tried to exterminate the Jewish people. He was merely another in a long line of corrupt people that Satan has used to try to wipe the Jews off the face of the earth. Satan hates the Jews passionately because they are God's chosen people, the race through which the Messiah came into the world. There could be (and have been) whole books written on this subject, and it's not my intention to go into the situation any more than I already have, except to say that Satan is

---

[16] Globalfronteirmissiongroups.com, "Unreached People Groups – Global Frontier Missions," Copyright 2023

thwarted at every turn. What he intends for evil, God uses for good.

Nearly 200 years before Judah was defeated by the Babylonians, Israel fell to the Assyrians and thousands of people were forcibly removed from their homeland. In the aftermath of these tragedies, thousands of Jews spread out around the world, settling throughout Africa, Asia and Europe, and later in North and South America. Since World War II and the atrocities committed by Adolf Hitler and the Nazis, millions of Jews from around the world are finding their way back to Israel. This is a fulfillment of prophecies that were given thousands of years ago about what would happen in the end times.

The prophet Isaiah said, *"He will raise a flag among the nations and assemble the exiles of Israel. He will gather the scattered people of Judah from the ends of the earth"* (Isaiah 11:12).

Jeremiah added, *"Return home, you wayward children,"* s ays the LORD, *"for I am your master. I will bring you back to the land of Israel--one from this town and two from that family--from wherever you are scattered'* (Jeremiah 3:14).

And, *"Listen to this message from the LORD, you nations of the world; proclaim it in distant coastlands: The Lord, who scattered his people, will gather them and watch over them as a shepherd does his flock"* (Jeremiah 31:10).

God also spoke through Ezekiel about this: *"This is what the Sovereign* LORD *says: The people of Israel will again live in their own land, the land I gave my servant Jacob. For I will gather them from the distant lands where I have scattered them. I will reveal to the nations of the world my holiness among my people"* (Ezekiel 28:25).

This is just a sampling of the many verses that speak of the Jews returning to Israel in the Last Days. These prophecies are being fulfilled right before our eyes. God used Moses to bring the Israelites out of Egypt and back to the Holy Land. Later, he used Ezra, Nehemiah and others to bring His people back from captivity in Babylonia. Now, He, Himself is bringing them back to Israel from countries all over the world. The stage is being set for fulfillment of this dramatic prophecy from the prophet Zechariah: *"Then I will pour out a spirit of grace and prayer on the family of David and on the people of Jerusalem. They will look on me whom they have pierced and mourn for him as for an only son. They will grieve bitterly for him as for a firstborn son who has died"* (Zechariah 12:10).

He is coming soon

Based on all the signs we have just talked about, I believe that Christ's return is imminent. At the same time, I also know that with God, "One day is like one thousand years and one thousand years is like a day" (2 Peter 3:8).

I also believe that before the end comes, there will be a great revival. When we speak about revival, we refer to a spiritual awakening, as we discussed in the first chapter in this book. The Hebrew word for this is *ḥāyāh* (*anadsaō* in Greek) and both of these words literally mean coming back to life from the dead. It's the awakening of hearts converted to the Father, motivated by God, that brings about the full restoration of men.

Revival is a new life. This is why we believe that God will continue to awaken hearts, and the evidence of this will be reflected in care for orphans and widows, respect for seniors, visits to the sick and those who are confined in prisons, nursing homes or their own homes. Revival ignites love in hearts and causes us to want to reach out to the lost and lonely in the name of Jesus. And, as we reach out in His name, revival expands and grows and is ignited in even more hearts.

I heard about one community where one of the residents was seriously ill. A neighboring family promised to pray for him on a daily basis and asked another family to join them. That family asked another, and so on. Soon, these prayer warriors began gathering every night to pray for their ailing friend. Some of these people had never been in each other's homes before, but now they were opening up their homes and their hearts to each other as the "prayer group" moved throughout the neighborhood. The gatherings included people from many different denominations, including some who had never been inside a church before and had never heard the gospel. The nightly prayer sessions blossomed into a neighborhood revival, which continues as I write this. Yes, it is amazing what God can and will do.

We cannot confirm we are in a spiritual revival if the earth does not give signs to it. The first evidence of a personal revival is when you decide to let your old self die so that God's perfect will can manifest itself in you. The evidence of a true revival in a church or faith community is when we can see in every service people reconciling their hearts with the Lord, converting to Christ, when the prayer for the sick doesn't pass by like a simple announcement, and the people congregated there start to live in sanctity until the return of our Savior. Just as our Lord told us: *"'You must love the* LORD *your God with all your heart, all your soul, and all your mind.' This is the first and greatest commandment. A second is equally important: 'Love your neighbor as yourself.' The entire law and all the demands of the prophets are based on these two commandments." (Matthew 22:27-40)*

Revival starts with love; love toward God, our neighbors, and ourselves. For revival to be present in your life, it has to start with the desire for God's Word. The Bible is not just a collection of old stories and inspirational quotes, but it is our guide to live a victorious life in Christ and the key that opens the door to revival. Nehemiah 8:5–6, says: *"All the people saw Ezra open the book, for he was standing above all of them. And all the people stood up when he opened it. Then Ezra gave honor and thanks to the Lord the great God. And all the people answered, "Let it be so!" while lifting up their hands. They bowed low with their faces to the ground and worshiped the Lord."*

When the people stood in the plaza to listen to the Word of God, they cried because of their sins that led them to such shameful circumstances. But once they repented, it was time to worship God, rejoice in His strength, and celebrate His goodness, mercy, and grace. When Ezra read the book of the law, the people of Israel listened, honored, paid attention, and acted on God's Word. The people devoted themselves to God completely.

God's will for your life and mine is for us to enjoy our faith and experience the joy of a vital relationship with Him. When we surrender everything we are, we gain everything God is. If we truly comprehend the practical power as described in this book, we will be transformed to cause an impact in this world. Will you please pray with me?

> *Lord, thank you for these principles and the revival found in Ezra. Help me put them in practice in my own life so that I can be more like Christ for your glory and the growth of your kingdom. I ask you in the name of Jesus. Amen.*

Lesson #12 from the Book of Ezra

Would you like to start a revival in your church or community? It starts by listening to God, as Ezra did, and looking for opportunities to share His love and His Word! Go to Him in prayer, asking Him to ignite a revival and to show you how you can be a part of it. It's also important to ask your Christian friends or neighbors to pray with you. As the Bible says, "If two of you agree here on earth concerning anything you ask, my Father in heaven will do it for you.' (Matthew 18:19) Another important key to revival is confession of sin, repentance and demonstrating love for your neighbor. Love is powerful and contagious. I believe that love for our neighbors builds love for God. And where people are open and receptive to God's love, revival breaks out.

QUESTIONS FOR SPIRITUAL REFLECTION

1. When was the last time you made a pact with God? What was the nature of that pact?

____

____

____

2. Have you experienced the liberty that God gives through the confession of sins? How did this experience change your life?

____

____

____

3. Is there anything in your life that stands between you and a right relationship with God? If so, what will you do about it?

____

____

____

4. Have you confessed Jesus as your Lord and Savior? If not, will you do it right now?

____

____

____

5. What does revival look like in your intimacy with God?

____

____

____

STEP INTO THE KINGDOM

BEFORE WE END OUR TIME TOGETHER, I WANT TO speak to anyone who has not yet accepted Jesus Christ as his or her Lord and Savior. If you surrender your life to Jesus, He will cleanse you of all your sins and restore your life, just as He restored Jerusalem after her destruction at the hands of the Babylonian army. Jerusalem and her great temple were reduced to a pile of rubble, but our Lord restored them to their former beauty and majesty. You may feel like your life has been reduced to a pile of rubble. Your once-beautiful dreams have been crushed by disappointment. You feel that you have let so many people down. If so, Jesus will forgive you, restore you, and help you become the person you always wanted to be.

On the other hand, you may feel that your life is going along just fine. You may feel fulfilled and satisfied. If so, I guarantee you that when Jesus comes into your life, He will give you such joy and peace that you will wonder how you ever got along before. Whoever you are, whatever your state in life, accepting Jesus as your Lord and Savior will make things so much better. You will have a purpose in life. A friend who loves you at all times. A Savior who will lift you up whenever you fall and put your feet back on solid ground.

And all you have to do is pray a simple prayer, confessing that you are a sinner and that you want to surrender your life to Jesus. You can use the following prayer as a pattern, although I urge you to put into your own words. Don't worry if you feel tongue-tied and struggle to find the right words. He understands how you feel and He knows your heart.

Here are five verses from the Bible to support what I am saying:

"I [Jesus] am the way, the truth, and the life. No one can come to the Father except through me" (John 14:6)"

"Anyone who believes in God's Son has eternal life. Anyone who doesn't obey the Son will never experience eternal life but remains under God's angry judgment" (John 3:36)."If you openly declare that Jesus is Lord and believe in your heart that God raised him from the dead, you will be saved" (Romans 10:9).

"Whoever has the Son has life; whoever does not have God's Son does not have life" (1 John 5:12).

"Look! I [Jesus] stand at the door and knock. If you hear my voice and open the door, I will come in, and we will share a meal together as friends"(Revelation 3:20).

I urge you to make a decision to accept Christ now. You can use the following prayer to guide you as you pray:

Dear Heavenly Father, thank you for sending your Son Jesus Christ to earth to give His life as a sacrifice for my sins. I believe that Jesus took upon Himself the punishment I deserve, that He was crucified in my behalf, that his broken body was placed in a tomb, and that He came back to life on the Third Day. I also believe that through Him I am victorious over sin and death. I accept Him as my Lord and Savior and ask you to help me follow your plan for my life. Thank you for your love and mercy and for the free gift of eternal life. I pray this all in the precious name of Jesus Christ. Amen